# Mamaleh Knows Best

# Mamaleh Knows Best

WHAT JEWISH MOTHERS DO

TO RAISE SUCCESSFUL,

CREATIVE,

EMPATHETIC,

INDEPENDENT CHILDREN

## MARJORIE INGALL

**HARMONY**

BOOKS · NEW YORK

Library of Congress Cataloging-in-Publication Data
Names: Ingall, Marjorie.
Title: Mamaleh knows best : what Jewish mothers do to raise successful,
    creative, empathetic, independent children / Marjorie Ingall.
Description: First Edition. | New York : Harmony, 2016. | Includes
    index.
Identifiers: LCCN 2016010796| ISBN 9780804141413 (hardback) |
    ISBN 9780804141420 (eISBN)
Subjects: LCSH: Parenting. | Child rearing—Religious aspects—
    Judaism. | BISAC: FAMILY & RELATIONSHIPS / Parenting
    / General. | RELIGION / Judaism / General. | FAMILY &
    RELATIONSHIPS / General.
Classification: LCC HQ755.8 .I54 2016 | DDC 649/.1—dc23
    LC record available at https://lccn.loc.gov/2016010796

ISBN 978-0-8041-4141-3
eBook ISBN 978-0-8041-4142-0

Printed in the United States of America

Jacket design by Elena Giavaldi
Jacket illustration by Luci Gutiérrez

10 9 8 7 6 5 4 3 2 1

First Edition

*For Carol K. Ingall—my moral
and awesomeness exemplar*

# CONTENTS

# Mamaleh Knows Best

# INTRODUCTION

First learn, then teach.

*—Yiddish proverb*

I was not an easy child. I was scared of my own shadow. I was a know-it-all. I was rabidly self-righteous. I did poorly with anything new. My mom once dropped me off for a class in magic—I loved magic!—at my local library. We were two minutes late and they'd started a handkerchief trick before I got there, and I panicked and ran back out the door after my mom, sobbing. I was probably eight or nine—far too old to be such a nervous *chaleria*. (Now might be a good time to tell you there's a Yiddish glossary in the back of the book.) I sobbed when my parents left me at camp. To be honest, I sobbed when my parents left me at college.

I was a button pusher. At my Orthodox Jewish day school, I insisted that Adam and Eve couldn't have been real people. Or if they were, they must have been cavemen, with heavy brow ridges and minimal chins. (I'd read about Neanderthals somewhere that was *not* my school library.) I got sent to the principal's office for this heresy. Another time, I asked the rabbi who taught our prayer class why the girls in our school had to stand in the back of the auditorium behind a wall, known as a *mechitza*. (Some Orthodox Jews believe in separating the genders during prayer.) I wasn't happy with the answer I got—that using a barrier served to protect everyone's focus and helped everyone pray better—so I led the girls in my class in getting as close to the wall as we could and singing and murmuring in prayer as loudly as we could. The rabbi was furious, but I looked at him with innocent doe eyes. We were *praying*! What could he do?

I came by troublemaking honestly. My dad was always a provocateur—an antinuclear activist willing to get arrested for his beliefs, a naughty joke teller, a writer of mischievous letters of complaint to large corporations. When he almost died of a heart attack at thirty-nine, he wrote an ethical will for my little brother, Andy, and me. His primary piece of advice: "Never, never take anything too seriously. Especially yourself."

He went on:

*I am so proud of you. I would not want better children. I would like you to do the following:*

*Be what you choose.*

*Help other people, whether this is your work or not. This is critical to the survival of Man and the worth of Man in this world—help other people. Help other people to feel good about themselves. That gives you a wonderful feeling, too.*

*Belch loudly at the dinner table. It is a compliment to the chef, and a long-established Ingall tradition. Teach your children this above all.*

*Always laugh and sing and make music.*

Other than choosing a gender-neutral pronoun instead of "Man," I really can't imagine better advice. (Well, maybe to be selective about the belching.) My dad died at sixty-four—much too young—but I reread his ethical will at least once a year. It makes me smile.

My mom is thankfully still here. She's more respectful of authority than my dad ever was, more deliberate and thoughtful, and more interested in doing the hard work of learning. When I was little, she was the director of our state's Bureau of Jewish Education, and then in her fifties she got her doctorate in education. She ultimately became a superstar professor at the Jewish Theological Seminary. She taught me about Jewish feminism, about great Jewish women throughout history, about how Jewish texts reflect powerful and often universal ethics.

When I had a kid of my own, suddenly I was faced with a little girl as contrary and bright and willful as I'd been. (My mom often chortles when I share child-rearing stories, saying, "You're getting yours!") I started considering how to raise a person who reflected the best of both my parents—a reader, a thinker, a person who stood up against injustice, but one with my mom's savvy rather than my dad's bull-in-a-china-shop mode.

Make no mistake: Josie was ferocious. She was a tiny playground thug and a two-year-old who spent much of her nursery school day in the Consequences Chair. I was, frankly, a little afraid of her. Sometimes I felt like my best parenting strategy was to pretend she was a Doberman: Don't show fear.

I didn't know what I was doing. I didn't read parenting books. But I often thought of the Jewish stories and history I was raised with, and I realized that they served as brilliant parenting advice. When Maxie was born, she was infinitely mellower and more easygoing than her sister. And I discovered that Jewish wisdom worked as well for raising a chill little comedian as it did for a tightly wound, competitive little warrior. "Each child carries their own blessings into the world," says the Yiddish proverb. Being a good parent means being flexible enough to see each child's individual blessings.

When Josie was a baby, I started writing a parenting column for the venerable Jewish newspaper *The Forward,* called "The East Village Mamele" (that was the paper's preferred way of spelling the Yiddish word that means "little mama," a term of endearment). After seven biblical years, I moved to *Tablet,* an edgier and more literary Jewish publication.

For a long time I enjoyed writing about my kids. I wrote wince-inducing odes to the smell of baby Josie's head, gushed about Maxie's riotous halo of curls, and pontificated about excess materialism, permissiveness, and bad children's television. I also wrote earnest and dippy pieces for American parenting magazines, generally following the mandatory format of (1) gosh-this-parenting-thing-is-hard-and-full-of-effluvia-and-dirty-laundry followed by (2) and-then-my-baby-smiled-her-delicious-gummy-smile-and-nothing-else-mattered. (This kind of parenting writing is a stage, like teething.)

When I wrote about my babies, I was really writing about myself. But as my kids got older, I got less and less comfortable sharing stories about them. As they developed self-consciousness, self-control, anxieties, passions, and their own ethical struggles, I started to feel their stories weren't mine to tell. So when my kids were seven and ten, I made the choice not to write about them unless I had their permission. (Josie vetted this manuscript. Maxie waved her arm airily and said, "Knock yourself out, lady. I trust you.")

For many mothers of all backgrounds, writing is a way to process the challenges of parenting, to vent, and to gain insight into our own behavior and that of our kids. I'm hardly the first on this road. Allow me to introduce you to another Jewish mother-slash-writer who filled multiple diaries. (Me, I fill Facebook.) This woman led an eventful life—married young, had kids, and balanced work and family and had a good sense of humor about it all. She and her husband were madly in love; they were intellectual and emotional peers. He shared all the details of his successful import-export business with her, and she helped him run it. She advised him, helped craft contracts, kept the books. Sadly, he died young, of sepsis. When he was asked whether he had any final requests, he murmured, "My wife knows everything."

Suddenly our diarist was a widowed mother in her early forties. That was when she started writing, to "stifle and banish the melancholic thoughts which came to me during many sleepless nights." She took over her husband's business and grew it to many times its original size, traveling to stock exchanges and markets throughout Europe and Russia, becoming very, very wealthy. Her kids grew to adulthood, married well, had careers and families of their own.

Some gave her trouble; most didn't. Her diaries brimmed with moral lessons: her belief in the importance of education and ethical business dealings, her stories about work and the joy and fulfillment she found in the act of writing.

This diarist was named Glückel of Hameln. Her diaries are now almost three hundred years old. But her writing is as relevant now as it was when she churned it out in the late seventeenth and early eighteenth centuries. It's the perfect encapsulation of Jewish motherhood throughout the ages, illustrating the values that make us who we are.

Glückel's diaries show us how Jewish mothers have historically prized education, spirituality, and ritual; how we believe in fostering independence and personal responsibility in our children; how we want our kids to live ethical lives full of acts of social justice. Her work shows how strongly we believe that mothers should work if they wish to or need to, that women are entitled to intellectual and spiritual lives apart from their offspring. Jewish women have always been engaged in *parnassa v'chalkalah*—livelihood and sustenance—of our own. And like Glückel, we've always had a Talmudic love of words, lecturing, hectoring, debating, and arguing. In these respects, not much has changed between the late 1600s and today.

When Glückel was widowed, she had eight children still living at home. (She had twelve in all. You are a slacker.) But she did what she had to do; after the requisite thirty days of mourning, she paid the bills, auctioned off parts of the business, dealt with creditors, and began rebuilding. She ultimately became the Spanx entrepreuneuse of her day, adding silk stockings to her husband's roster of gems, precious metals, and money exchange. She did business in Amsterdam, Berlin, Leipzig, and Paris, often traveling to locations—like the Hamburg Bourse—deemed too dangerous for women.

Glückel's narrative tone zigzagged dizzyingly between self-dramatizing and self-deprecating. She berated herself for not writing more faithfully, then noted with ironic self-awareness that uh, she had little kids. New motherhood made her feel—and here you can almost hear the sardonic tone—"more heavily burdened than anyone else in the world, and that no one suffered from their children as much as I." Sometimes she obsessed about money and *kvetch*ed like a Germanic Fran Drescher. But she also told ghost stories and gossiped like the person you'd definitely want to sit next to at a Bat Mitzvah.

In short, Glückel is a far cry from the stereotype of the Jewish mother as demanding, shallow, boastful, monstrously narcissistic, and clingy. *("What's the difference between a Jewish mother and a Rottweiler? A Rottweiler eventually lets go.")*

This hateful stereotype came to its fullest flower back in the '60s to '80s, when there was a mania for Jewish mother jokes—along with blond jokes, Polish jokes, and Jewish American Princess jokes. These nuggets of hilarity are in large part what contributed to the widespread stereotype of Jewish mothers as the original helicopter parents: clingy, needy, guilt-mongering hovercraft who always believe their precious spawn are perfect.

The stereotype isn't reality. It was the creation of a specific time and place in history, one we'll talk about more in Chapter 1. Widen the lens and you'll see a much broader perspective on Jewish motherhood, across countries and centuries, than this wee stretch of American history suggests. And it just so happens that Jewish parenting methods are in line with modern research on fostering children's creativity, kindness, and intellect. They're why Jews have been so successful over the years. There's a reason that even though we make up less than 1 percent of the world's population, we also constitute:

- 170 of the 850 Nobel Prize winners
- 21 percent of Ivy League students
- 26 percent of Kennedy Center honorees
- 37 percent of Academy Award–winning directors
- 51 percent of Pulitzer Prize winners for nonfiction

We're not just talking modern American history here. Let's go back to the Middle Ages. From 1150 to 1350, 95 of the 626 known scientists working everywhere in the world were Jews. (That stat comes courtesy of goyish historian of science George Sarton.) These numbers are obviously way out of proportion to the Jewish population. According to the data crunching of conservative political scientist Charles Murray, Jewish representation in European literature from 1870 to 1950 was four times the number one would expect given Europe's Jewish population. In music, the degree of overrepresentation was five times. In biology, eight times. In physics, nine times. In mathematics, twelve times. In philosophy, fourteen times. (Rest assured that this is the last time in the book I will quote conservative political scientist Charles Murray.)

I don't need some other guy's statistics to prove that Jewish-style parenting fosters not just success, but also menschiness. (A *mensch* is a Yiddish term for a good, ethical person.) Historical sources show that Jewish-style child-rearing is good not only for kids, but also for parents. Texts as disparate as the Torah (the Five Books of Moses, known to many non-Jews as the Old Testament), the Talmud (a compendium of Jewish law and commentary), medieval prayers and letters, seventeenth-century spiritual writings, nineteenth-century British and American educational philosophy, and narratives by Jewish mothers throughout history tell the story that true Jewish motherhood is not self-negating or martyring. It values women's intellectual and emotional lives, which benefits the culture as a whole. And it leads to hardworking, creative, independent kids.

I'm going to say it straight out: *Jewish parenting methods are responsible for the outsized success of the Jewish people.* But to paraphrase the old Levy's rye bread slogan, you don't have to be Jewish to be a Jewish mother.

In the first chapter of this book, I'll talk a bit about where the wrongheaded stereotype of the Jewish mother came from. (Skip it if you just want me to tell you what to do and you're an eat-dessert-first kind of person.) In the succeeding nine chapters, I'll offer historical background, personal anecdotes, and strategies from Jewish texts to show readers of all faiths how to implement Jewish mothering practices in their own lives and raise more self-sufficient, ethical, and accomplished kids.

Think of Glückel, and read on.

## Chapter 1

# Know Your History

How do we know Jesus was Jewish? He lived at home with his mother until he was thirty, went into his father's business, and had a mother who thought he was God.

—*Really old joke*

When I had babies, I hated being called Mama. (When the pediatrician airily did it—or called me Mother or Mommy—I wanted to use the snotsucker bulb on him.) I think to a degree I disliked it because it negated me as a person. It turned me into the vessel, the baby wearer, the stroller pusher, the milk source. It made me feel like a featureless feeder from a sci-fi flick. But I also shuddered because I had internalized certain stereotypes about what being a Jewish mother, specifically, meant.

The Jewish mother stereotype isn't pretty. It depicts someone needy, neurotic, clingy—a guilt-shooting laser whose entire identity comes from her children (preferably her son who is a doctor and her daughter who marries one). I had to process why, precisely, the words *Jewish mother* made me shudder—why I'd personalized this stereotype. I had to learn what the truth was, and where the cliché came from. For us to understand why Jewish parenting has worked so well throughout history—and has been so underheralded as the reason for Jews' outsize success—we need to look at who the world thinks the Jewish mother is. Then we can look more closely at who she really is and what she's done so right.

Today, the most prominent old-school Jewish mother might be Kyle Broflovski's mom, Sheila, on *South Park*— fat, loud, with a New Jersey accent and helmet hair, perpetually spluttering in outrage, "What, What, WHAT?" and kvetching about anti-Semitism. Then there's Judith Light's narcissistic, neurotic Shelly Pfefferman on *Transparent,* and Tovah Feldshuh's mother to Rachel Bloom's *Crazy Ex-Girlfriend,* belting an aria of criticism and guilt ("By the way you're looking healthy / and by healthy I mean chunky / I don't mean that as an insult / I'm just stating it as fact . . . I see your eczema is back!"). Until 2015, there was Howard Wolowitz's mother on *The Big Bang Theory,* a guilt-hurling, soul-crushing, son-infantilizing, housecoat-wearing, Yiddish-inflected force of nature, perpetually bellowing at her progeny from somewhere offscreen.

These characters come from a long tradition of funny and not-so-funny jokes and stereotypes. Today, we Jews are primarily perceived as regular boring white people, but once we were considered pre-Tiger-Mother Tiger Mothers. Back in the day, Catskills comics got endless material from the notion of Jewish mothers as suffocating, whining, melodramatic, demanding grief givers.

Q. What did the waiter ask the table of Jewish mothers?
A. Is ANYTHING all right?

A Jewish mother is walking down the street with her two little sons. A passerby says, "Oh, they're so cute! How old are they?" The Jewish mother responds, "The doctor is three and the lawyer is two."

Q. Why do Jewish mothers make great parole officers?
A. They never let anyone finish a sentence.

A lot of these Jewish mother jokes have the schticky rhythms of the Borscht Belt, a lost world of Jewish resorts where many American comics got their start or performed regularly. (Among them: Woody Allen, Lenny Bruce, Rodney Dangerfield, Phyllis Diller, Jerry Lewis, Zero Mostel, Carl Reiner, Don Rickles, Joan Rivers, and Jerry Stiller. To name a few.) But while performers in these hotels mocked Jewish mothers, the hotels themselves were often *run* by Jewish mothers. That's where we start to see the truth behind the stereotype. And that's what I think is worth emulating.

## A QUICK PRIMER ON THE HISTORICAL (NOT HYSTERICAL) JEWISH MOTHER

For great swaths of Jewish history, men studied and women worked.

Jews valued brains because brains were all we had. We were a wandering people. Throughout recorded history, pretty much every time Jews got comfortable, they wound up getting booted from whatever country they were living in. Jews were expelled from England in the thirteenth century, France and Hungary in the fourteenth, Austria and Spain and Portugal in the fifteenth, just for starters. Hasidic folktales are full of wanderers, of lessons taught in motion. So much of Jewish identity has been tied to feeling homeless, worrying about where it's safe to lay one's hat. The anxiety is right there in our ancient texts, and it's in what actually happened to us throughout history. Every period of comfort and luxury was followed by a massacre or an expulsion. Jews learned that it was difficult to trust good times and good things.

For many centuries in many countries, Jews were forbidden to own land, barred from many professions, subject to discriminatory laws and taxes. When circumstances are awful and uncertain, the things you can rely on are internal: wit, literacy, and spirituality. So men studied—doing the thing that Jews truly cherished. Which is great, but someone had to put bread on the table. That meant that while men were scholars, women were often the breadwinners. In tough times, mamalehs stepped up.

But times were not always tough. While most people (Jews included) think of Jewish history as an endless string of pogroms and persecution, there were numerous time periods in various countries in which being a Jew did not suck. In these good times, Jewish women owned property, pleaded causes in court, created art, wrote their own prayer books, ran big businesses. They raised children who became prominent philosophers, composers, novelists, merchants, scientists, philanthropists.

In the sixth and fifth centuries BCE (Before the Common Era—many Jews don't use the term "BC," what with Christ not being our particular guy) some Jews lived pretty luxurious lives. Egyptian Jews had snazzy homes, were worldly and acculturated lives, and liked nice clothes. Jews in Jerusalem muttered that they were insufficiently religious and too prone to intermarry. (Muttering about other Jews being insufficiently religious is still a common Jewish pastime today.) Similarly, at different times in Persia, the Hellenistic world, Spain and Portugal, Germany, France and England, Jews lived urban and urbane lives in which they associated with their non-Jewish neighbors and enjoyed the fruits of majority culture.

Jewish women had political and economic power from the very beginning of recorded history. On the Egyptian island of Elephantine, a woman named Mibtahiah, born in 476 BCE, owned her own house. She married twice and allowed both husbands to use her home, which was sweet of her.

In wildly different environments—both hostile and welcoming—Jewish mothers managed to support their families, emotionally and economically, and raise impressive, creative, highly educated, and ambitious kids. They were clearly doing something right. Don't we want to do the same?

## THE AMERICAN JEWISH MOTHER

Yet somehow, after World War II, the Jewish mother became an object of mockery. A confluence of factors was responsible: Jews started to move to the burbs, the promised land of lawns and *goyim*. Jewish sons began to learn to talk like cultured Americans while their (superembarrassing) mothers retained their ethnic Old Country speaking rhythms. Jewish mothers reeled from the horrifying news of the deaths of six million Jews overseas and reacted, perhaps, with more than usual clinginess toward their own children.

Indeed, I don't think you can overstate the psychological repercussions of the Holocaust. Jews throughout the country saw the gulf between their own affluent lives and the recent obliteration of Jewish worlds an ocean away. There's a kernel of truth in many stereotypes . . . including that of the Jewish mother. I'm certainly willing to believe that Jewish mothers in the 1950s and 1960s clung a little more tightly to their children. I suspect that post-Holocaust anxiety was part of why the Jewish mother became a caricature, paired with American Jews experiencing a time of increasing suburbanization, assimilation, and Jewish economic advancement.

But the stereotype *really* gained traction because of the changing media landscape. American Jewish male writers—freed in an age of antiheroic literature to tell their own kinds of stories—created squawking, controlling Jewish mother characters. TV picked up the stereotypes and broadcast them further. In the 1950s, 77 percent of American households purchased their first TV. Suddenly Jewish boys with mama issues had what today's media *machers* call a platform.

This time period also coincided with the rise of the nebbishy, antiheroic voice in fiction. Suddenly a lot of youngish Jewish male writers had the voice and opportunity to express their own autobiographical *mishegas* about their mothers. Writers like Herman Wouk, Philip Roth, and Saul Bellow and jokesters like Woody Allen and Jackie Mason wrote with varying levels of sexism and conflicted feelings about their moms. Basically, here we have a bunch of nerdy guys coming of age in an era in which Jews are rapidly melded into wider society while still feeling like outsiders. In their books and comedy routines, they created semiautobiographical characters and literary stand-ins who yearned for a less annoying, less domineering, less kvetchy mom who was better able to "blend." They frequently blamed women for their own feelings of displacement and inadequacy in America.

When I was little, my Bubbe had a book called *How to Be a Jewish Mother,* first published in 1965. It was by a humorist named Dan Greenburg, and as a little kid I thought it was hilarious. I liked the pictures, depicting what to wear to go in the water so as not to drown and how to make a wildly overstuffed sandwich so your children do not starve. There were sections called "Making Guilt Work," "The Technique of Basic Suffering," and "Seven Basic Sacrifices to Make for Your Child." (Greenburg's book pointed out, just as this one does, that "you don't have to be either Jewish or a mother to be a Jewish mother. An Irish waitress or an Italian barber could also be a Jewish mother." Jewish motherhood is a philosophy, not an identity!) The book offered advice like "Let your child hear you sigh every day; if you don't know what he's done to make you suffer, *he* will." And "Don't let him know you fainted twice in the supermarket from fatigue. But make sure he knows you're not letting him know."

From the '50s to the '80s, pop culture was full of jokes like these, snarking at Jewish mothers for being overprotective, ethnocentric, and full of braggy bloviation about their spawn. Such jokes reflect American anxiety about values, and it's always easy to blame the mother. Are we worried that children are too materialistic? Are we freaked about our compatriots not being religiously observant enough? BLAME

THE MOTHER! (Needless to say, "blame the mother" is not an exclusively Jewish response. Recall the Cleveland police officer whose social media response to the death of local twelve-year-old, toy-gun-holding Tamir Rice was "Raise your kids not to play with fake guns, you stupid bitch.")

To be fair, Jews have often been embarrassed and horrified by women in general, not just mothers. (Go, us.) The very entertaining historian Jenna Weissman Joselit has written about Jewish anxiety regarding the "Ghetto Girl"—a tacky, working-class young woman wearing too much makeup, too obsessed with clothes, talking too loudly. There are references to her as early as the turn of the twentieth century. The bestselling (secular Jewish) novelist Fannie Hurst blamed the Ghetto Girl's brassiness on "the vivid, aggressive temperament and imagination of the Jew." And yet! Even these janky, classless types often managed to rise above their station, to the bafflement of the haters. "When I go down to the East Side and look upon those pasty, white faces and hopelessly vulgar, stupid dresses," Hurst wrote loftily, "I am filled with wonder and admiration that these girls, with all their vulgarity, should rise to the heights that some of them do and be so great in achievement." Being horrified at young women's clothing and manners and shocked at their accomplishments never goes out of style.

The Ghetto Girl stereotype evolved into the Jewish American Princess stereotype . . . which is the flip side of the Jewish American Mother stereotype. Folklorist Alan Dundes, who studied jokes related to both, referred to them as the JAM and the JAP. The JAM was extravagantly self-negating, obsessed with feeding her family, unable to let go of her progeny. The JAP was all about glittering surfaces—selfish, shallow, emotionally uninvested in her fellow human beings, obsessively manicure oriented. *(What does a JAP make for dinner? Reservations.)* Opposites, see? But both the JAM and the JAP were emotional and economic vampires, and both were a reflection of ingrained misogyny.

Because weirdly, as jokes and books that mocked insular, tribal, nonworking Jewish women proliferated, Jewish women's participation in the labor force actually *rose*. Sociologist Riv-Ellen Prell noted that in 1957, 26 percent of American Jewish women between the ages of 25 and 34 and 34 percent of women between the ages of 35 and 44 were in the workforce. In 1990, 76 percent of women between the ages of 25 and 34 and 75 percent of women between the ages of 35 and 44 were in the workforce. What this means is that while Jewish men were portraying Jewish women as dependent moochers, Jewish women were actually returning to the workplace, which is where, over the span of world history, they spent much of their time anyway.

## YOO HOO, MRS. GOLDBERG!

You know who didn't mock Jewish mothers? *Jewish mothers.* The earliest Jewish mother in American pop culture, Molly Goldberg, was created by a woman, Gertrude Berg, and was portrayed with far more affection—both on the radio from 1929 to 1949 and on TV from 1949 to 1955—than the later, more grasping and grotesque Jewish mothers created by young Jewish men.

Berg was the matriarch of *The Goldbergs,* a fictional Jewish family led by a strong mother. Molly Goldberg was a busybody, but she was kind and a problem solver—the warm, competent head of a functional, loving family. She wasn't a supporting character, like later Jewish mothers on TV (such as Sophie Steinberg on *Bridget Loves Bernie,* Ida Morgenstern on *Rhoda,* Helen Seinfeld on *Seinfeld,* Sylvia Buchman on *Mad About You,* Sylvia Fine on *The Nanny,* and Bobbi Adler on *Will and Grace*). She was the *lead.* And I don't think it's accidental that her creator was female. That's precisely why she wasn't a cartoon, why she had so much more nuance than her successors in televised Jewish momdom. There's a Yiddish proverb that says, "A Jew is 28 percent fear, 2 percent sugar, and 70 percent chutzpah." That's Mrs. Goldberg. The caricatures who followed her lacked both the sweetening of sugar and the humanizing of fear. They were 100 percent *chutzpah*—mostly chutzpah that wasn't cute or charming. It wasn't aimed at helping their kids; it was narcissistic.

Hey, writers are as lazy as anyone else. (I know this for an actual fact.) Once the notion of the grasping Jewish mother had gained pop culture traction, it became short-hand—a frequently misogynistic way to telegraph *annoying-ness* and *otherness.* To be fair, mothers of a zillion cultures have been portrayed as noodgy and overbearing. We've seen demanding and withholding Tiger Moms, domineer-ing and high-pitched black moms, hectoring and screech-ing Hispanic moms. Apparently lots of guys have mommy issues. Yet the Jewish stereotype has gained more traction because Jews own the media. (I'm kidding.) (Mostly.)

## PUT DOWN THE LIVER

Perhaps the biggest single high-culture source for the Jew-ish mother stereotype is Philip Roth's novel *Portnoy's Com-*

*plaint*. It's hard to explain to a non-Jew just how much resonance this book has, and how much it has infuriated and distressed generations of Jewish women. (The book has its fans, of course. But as with the *Twilight* saga and *The Fountainhead*, there's no accounting for taste.) An NPR story on the book's fortieth anniversary noted, *"Portnoy's Complaint* did for the Jewish mother what *Jaws* did for the shark: Took an already frightening creature and made it even scarier."

The portrait of Sophie Portnoy solidified the notion of the Jewish mother as a horrifying force of nature, the most helicoptery of helicopter parents. She demands to see her adult son's bowel movements, kvetches endlessly, tries to control his romantic life, refuses to give him any kind of adult agency.

The book turned truth into a cartoon. Back when Jewish mothers lived in *shtetls* (small, pre-Holocaust Eastern European towns), to be a good *balaboosta,* a competent manager of the home, the Jewish mother had to be on top of everything—finances, budgeting, cooking, cleaning, child-rearing, marketing, perhaps running a business. Being in charge got things done. Being retiring and delicate did not. But Roth turned a grain of truth into a monstrosity. Sure, this is just one character in one book, but its influence is outsized.

## THE TROUBLE WITH BEING HAPPY

Today, American Jews seem to be living in the promised land. We win big literary awards and have cool jobs. People in this country have not tended to dump us in mass

graves. Jews have been granted dominion over their historical homeland, too; the modern State of Israel was founded
in 1948. (By the by, we are *not* talking Israeli politics in this
book. You want that, go read something else.) For a people
who've spent thousands of years seeing themselves as wanderers, what does it mean to have a home? Can we actually
chill out? And if we're actually in a place of ease and comfort where we can have meaningful leadership roles, how
do we maintain the energy, creativity, and drive that fueled
us for so much of our history as a people in exile? Can Jewish parenting continue to transmit the kind of solid values
and flexible thinking that has served Jews well in an ever-
changing, uncertain world? Are we doomed to lose the values and attributes that have made us so accomplished and
innovative for generations?

There are people who have no clue that there even *is* a
Jewish mother stereotype. In America today, Jewish mothers have become just plain American mothers. Through
the inevitable march of time and acculturation, the JAM—
along with the Ghetto Girl and the JAP—has receded from
popular consciousness. The Jewish mother as mythic figure
and punch line faded away pretty much around the time
*The Nanny* went off the air.

Tiger Mothers have taken the Jewish mother's place in
the cultural firmament, as yet another immigrant generation struggles to find its place in America. Chinese Americans are pretty much where we Jews were forty years ago.
This means there's a new female locus of love, suspicion,
fear, and resentment. While part of me is bummed to hand
over the comedic reins to other groups (especially since
we never even *saw* a wedding between a Jewish man and a
Jewish woman on a sitcom until *Will and Grace* in 2002, let

alone got to watch a youngish, non-harridan-esque Jewish mother raise her kids—come on! It's too soon for us to go!), the rest of me is fine with spreading the comedic wealth.

I think, though, the dearth of Jewish characters on network TV, despite the huge number of Jewish TV writers, is an indication that we're not quite sure who we are. We have spent so much time measuring ourselves against the majority culture. When we lived in a country and an era that was relatively accepting, we struggled to balance our Jewish identity with our participation in the wider world. When we lived in places and eras that hated us, we tried to keep our heads down, keep the faith, and do what we had to do to survive. Now, in a country and time of relative comfort, we're struggling to figure out who we're going to be in the next few generations. It's up to us Jews to be sure we don't slack in transmitting our historic values to our kids, giving them the tools they need to be successful. It's on us to continue to choose to be a "light unto the nations," the prophet Isaiah's term for the Jewish people's importance as role models for others. Right now, I'd argue that many Jews are losing touch with the morals and processes that have made our kids so successful in creative and scientific fields, in business, in journalism. We're forgetting what we once did that made our children do so brilliantly, in so many different cultures and countries, often while facing anti-Semitism and poverty.

But this isn't a book just for us. You don't need to be an Orthodox Jew or even a person who believes in God to raise a family with traditional Jewish values. Each of the following chapters of this book talks about what Jewish mothers have done over time to raise moral kids who can thrive in a complicated world.

## MIXING IT UP CAN BE GOOD FOR EVERYONE

My daughter Josie, at age two, wailed, "This is a disastrophe!" when our cat was dying. That was, indeed, a disastrophe. Jews have often worried that the future as a whole is a disastrophe. Many have predicted that living in a pluralistic world will cause the Death of the Jewish People. In 2013, the Pew Research Center released a report on the state of American Jewry that made many Jewish leaders run around squawking like Chicken Little. While the huge survey found that American Jews overwhelmingly said they were proud to be Jewish and had a strong sense of belonging to the Jewish people, many said they considered themselves Jews only by ethnicity or culture. Lots of us are no longer so into ritual or texts. And certainly—though not for the first time in our long history—rates of intermarriage are up. Yet I'd argue this doesn't spell the end of Judaism, or of Jewish values. In *'Til Faith Do Us Part,* a study of interfaith marriage, Naomi Schaefer Riley found that the *mother's faith* was the biggest factor in determining how families raised their children. A third of kids in interfaith families were being reared in their mother's religion, while only 15 percent were growing up in their father's.

Mothers have power. Women tend to be more religious than men (which is why Judaism, a largely home-based faith, has been not only practiced but also transmitted by women). Women are much more likely to go to religious services than men. And because mothers tend to be in charge of kids' schedules, women are the ones who ensure that religious education takes place.

I think living with diversity is good for us. Our once insular world is full of cracks, and as Leonard Cohen said, "That's how the light gets in." Being open to pluralism can lead to tolerance, a broader perspective on culture, greater human understanding. It's important for Jews—and people of all backgrounds—to know their history, stories, traditions, foods, music, art. Those who aren't Jewish can look to their own culture and family background for inspiration, while adapting Jewish values for raising modern kids. Just as an Irish waitress or an Italian barber can be a Jewish mother, so can anyone adapt Jewish tricks for raising flexible, quick-thinking, literate, open-minded kids. There are specific elements of Jewish child-rearing I think can be helpful to parents of all backgrounds, and they're what the rest of this book will explore.

If your own religious background doesn't feel relevant to your values, you still have family history to mine: How did your parents and grandparents and great-grandparents' views of the world affect your attitudes toward education, politics, conspicuous consumption, volunteering, people who aren't just like you? How do you want to emulate past generations . . . or how do you intend to be sure you don't, if you're not proud of your family's past? The storytelling we'll talk about in Chapter 7 can be a way to share family history, writ small or large, as well. Think about the Jewish value of chutzpah: smart-assedness, assertiveness, spunk, challenging authority, being willing to raise eyebrows and be a troublemaker. Independent thinking has served Jews well when authority couldn't be trusted. It's still what helps people create new scientific paradigms and forms of artistic expression today.

The stereotype of the Jewish mother was a product of a very particular place and time. It's not a reflection of five thousand years of Jewish history. Glückel's values—education, spirituality, honesty, and independence—are a better reflection of the teachings of the Jewish mother across time. These are the values all parents should emulate.

*Chapter 2*

# Nurture Independence— Your Kid's and Your Own

If each one sweeps before his own door, the whole street is clean.

*—Yiddish proverb*

When Josie and Maxie were nine and six, I started letting them walk to school alone. We lived one city block away from their school, on the opposite side of the street. This means they had to cross one street and one avenue to get there. I could watch from my building's stoop until they got to the corner and began crossing the street; I knew that on the other side the school crossing guard (Tina, who is a goddess) would help them cross the avenue.

People acted like I was sending them on the Bataan Death March.

Parents told me, accusingly, that they'd seen my kids walking alone. Had there been some family tragedy, some problem they could help with? Was I not worried about cars whipping around the corner and smacking them into next week? Wasn't I concerned about child snatchers? Once, a school aide who took issue with my decision literally refused to let Maxie leave the building and called me in disbelief, saying my child's safety was her paramount interest. I ordered her to let my kid go.

Yes, I had anxiety about this. Yes, I had still more anxiety after Josie graduated from fifth grade and Maxie began walking alone, at age seven. And yes, I sucked it up and let them go anyway.

Their road to pedestrian self-sufficiency was not without potholes. Once the two of them were in animated conversation and didn't look as they stepped into the street. A car honked; Tina, on the kitty-corner side of the avenue, bellowed at them. They scrambled back onto the curb, gasping. Tina berated them when they carefully got to her side. The next morning, I walked them, and Tina gave me an earful. Not about letting them go alone, but about making sure they always paid attention. Lesson learned, by all of us.

Another time, I was supposed to meet Maxie at school to take her to Hebrew school, but I forgot. Maxie waited on the corner with Tina, unsure about what to do. I remembered five minutes after I was supposed to be there and raced to school, full of apologies. Tina told me, "If something like this ever happens again, call me. I'll keep Maxie company or send her back into the school." She gave me her personal cell-phone number. (So nice, right?) After that, I gave Maxie house keys. Maxie felt big and responsible with her jingling ring of keys, and I felt reassured that I lived in a world in which other grown-ups were looking out for my kid. (I suspect you live in that world, too, even if you don't always ask for help, or believe it's out there. As our text *Pirkei Avot, Ethics of the Fathers,* says, *Al tifrosh min ha-tzibur;* don't separate yourself from the community. We can all be helpers and lean on each other.)

Kids need to learn independence. Studies have shown that encouraging kids' executive function (the ability to coordinate complex tasks and meet goals independently) early in life has great benefits down the road. We need good executive function to perform competently in the adult world, take the initiative on projects, organize our time, and work well with others. And having independence makes your kid happier. A 2011 North Carolina State University study found that kids whose parents try to direct their play (telling them how to build with LEGO, encouraging them to count squares in Candyland) felt more negative emotions than kids whose parents just let them be. When parents hover, as a 2013 study at the University of Missouri found, kids play less actively than when their parents back off. These findings are consistent—even among college students. A study by Holly Schiffrin at the University of Mary Washington in Virginia found that students "having over-controlling parents reported significantly higher levels of depression and less satisfaction with life." Other studies have shown that college students with overinvolved parents tended to feel less competent and less able to manage the stresses of life. They're also more likely to be depressed. In other words: Back the hell off.

It's our job as parents to relinquish control, bit by bit. Overprotective parenting is correlated with kids who are more likely to be depressed and bullied. If we don't let our kids be independent, we don't give them the chance to feel autonomous and proud of their own situation handling.

## HOW JUDAISM VALUES INDEPENDENCE

Despite the stereotype of the Jewish mother as an over-protective mollycoddler, we've historically been pretty good at encouraging our kids to make their own way in the world. The ancient Babylonian Talmud (code of law) says that parents have three obligations when it comes to child-rearing: Teach your kid Torah. Teach your kid to earn a living. And teach your kid to swim.

Wait, what? "What is the reason?" the Talmud queries. (This is the Talmud's way of saying "Wait, what?") "His life may depend on it." If we take this as metaphor, what this means is that you won't always be there to rescue your kid. You have to teach him to dog paddle, and then expect him to take it from there.

In Judaism we're fortunate to have a bar of independence set pretty early: the Bar or Bat Mitzvah. *Mitzvah* is the Hebrew word for commandment; a Bar or Bat Mitzvah is literally, a son or daughter of the commandment. When a kid is twelve or thirteen (depending on which branch of Judaism their family adheres to), they're expected to follow all the commandments in the Torah. Their family and community come together to say, "We welcome you as an adult, with all the rights and responsibilities this entails."

Of course we don't actually believe thirteen-year-olds are grown-ups. But the ritual is a way of announcing—to the kid, the family, and the wider world—that they're not dealing with a wee, unreliable, undependable, footloose-and-fancy-free child anymore. The family stands before the community saying, "Look! We have made an accountable human being!"

Coming-of-age ceremonies have of course been historically common in many cultures. The Amish have Rum-
springa, some Hispanic cultures have Quinceañeras,
Japanese families celebrate Seijin-no-Hi. The Sateré-Mawé
of the Brazilian Amazon initiate a boy into manhood by
having him wear a woven-leaf mitten filled with stinging
bullet ants. (Suddenly, reading a few verses of Torah sounds
like cake.) In anthropology the word *liminal* is used to mean
standing on the threshold, in a doorway, in a state of transition from one state to another. It's a sacred time of signifi-
cance and individuation. Bar and Bat Mitzvah codify the
importance of this transition.

But Jewish parents today sometimes forget that independence is a key value in our faith. Today most of us live
in a wider culture in which parents bail out their kids the
moment they get into a spot of trouble. And we ourselves
are generally in the fortunate position of being able to give
our kids significant assistance—practical, emotional, economic.

For generations, this wasn't the case. We weren't in a
position to hector teachers into giving our special snow-
flakes A+s or to use our professional savvy to get them
fabulous internships. We had no connections. We weren't
engaged in our kids' schooling because we didn't speak the
dominant language; our kids might not have gone very far
in school because we needed them to work to support the
family. In those days, we didn't have the kind of connections we do today, now that we run global banking and the
media. (I promise not to make this joke again. Maybe.)
Growing up in a genuinely scary world—one full of expul-
sions and pogroms and a Holocaust—tends to bring clarity
about the difference between real fears and manufactured

ones. When you have to worry about survival on a daily basis, you learn to tune out the *mishegas* of the small stuff.

## COMMON SENSE ABOUT RISK

Freaking out about the small stuff, in a way that is unsupported by data and logic, is a luxury. My friend Lenore Skenazy's blog *Free-Range Kids* ticks off and fact-checks examples of hysterical overparenting and paranoia: a parent insisting a nut tree on public property be cut down because it could cause breathing problems for her child with nut allergies; suburban parents getting picked up by cops for letting kids play outside unsupervised; schools banning tag, unsupervised cartwheels, and even running at recess. Recently Lenore looked at a study of urban, suburban, and rural neighborhoods in the United Kingdom, conducted by the Policy Studies Institute at the University of Westminster. It showed that in 1971, 80 percent of third graders walked to school alone. By 1990, the number had dropped to 9 percent. Today, it's even lower than that.

Our anxiety has grown in inverse proportion to the danger our kids are in. The truth is, cities are safer than they've been in years—way safer than they were when we were kids. According to the Bureau of Justice Statistics, violent crime in the United States has dropped 48 percent since 1993. In Canada, the crime rate has fallen steadily back to the level it was in 1972. In the United Kingdom, the murder rate is the lowest it's been since 1978. In Australia, the murder rate has declined by nearly a third since 1999.

We worry about kidnapping when we should worry about whether we're installing baby car seats properly. Kids abducted by strangers or slight acquaintances constitute *one hundredth of 1 percent* (that's 0.01%) of all missing children, according to the Center for Missing and Exploited Children, which estimates the actual number is around 115 a year. (That's around the same number as kids who die of the flu—most of whom are unvaccinated, by the way.) Our kids are in much more danger from family members and friends than from strangers. According to the U.S. Department of Justice, of all children under age five murdered from 1980 through 2008, 63 percent were killed by a parent, 28 percent by an acquaintance, 7 percent by another relative, and 3 percent by a stranger.

It's important to realize that most of us DO have people we can call in a crisis, and strangers tend to mensch it up when faced with a lost puppy or a kid in danger. But we keep choosing to believe the worst. In 1972, the General Social Survey (a demographic study conducted by the National Opinion Research Center at the University of Chicago) found that half of Americans believed that most people are trustworthy. By 2013, that number had fallen to one-third. Again, this growing mistrust has occurred at the same time that crime has fallen drastically. We are *choosing* to make squeaking noises and bug-eyed terrified faces like Beaker the Muppet.

Look, I won't deny that life—particularly city life—can be scary. The very first time we dropped nine-year-old Josie off in Brooklyn by herself—at a Studio in a School art class at Pratt Institute on a Sunday afternoon—we got stuck in traffic on the way back from Costco and were wildly late picking her up. We didn't know her teacher's name. We didn't have a phone number. Josie didn't yet have a cell phone. Because it was a program for public school kids run

in partnership with but not by Pratt, we had office numbers (but it was Sunday) and zero notion of whom to talk to
directly. We arrived forty minutes late. Josie's face was tear-
streaked and the college student who was teaching her class
wore the "OMG this is SO not what I signed up for" face.
But nothing terrible happened. The outcome was that we
got her a cell phone. Within the next year, she was walking
to flute lessons (eight and a half blocks away) and walking
or taking a bus to Hebrew school (nineteen blocks away) by
herself.

I will mildly point out that we hear a lot of privileged
parents bemoaning the way their kids are glued to their
phones, while failing to note that these same phones can
contribute to kids' freedom and ameliorate our own separation anxiety. Get a grip, people. (Incidentally, it is possible
to simultaneously be annoyed by a device and to appreciate that it has made life better. If you are annoyed by your
child's use of a device during family time, divest your child
of the phone during family time. This is not rocket science.
Incidentally, Jews have received fifty Nobel Prizes in physics, which is practically a Nobel in rocket science since there
is no actual Nobel in rocket science.)

We're all giving each other the side-eye, worrying that
other parents are judging us, worrying that our kid will be
that statistical outlier, worrying that someone will report us
to the cops as reckless or neglectful. (Reader, this last one
is not an idle fear. Once Maxie, then ten, was waiting for
the bus home after rehearsal for a play at our synagogue. It
was getting dark and chilly, but Maxie had a coat and the
neighborhood street was well trafficked, as usual. A busybody stopped Maxie at the bus stop to ask her name, where
she lived, where she was going, and where she'd come from.

Maxie, confused, told her. The next morning, the woman called the synagogue to report that she'd met a six-year-old girl named Maxie who had neglectful parents who needed to be dealt with. Thankfully, the education director who took her call told her that he knew our family and trusted our judgment. I think the woman meant well, in her way— she gave Maxie $20 for a taxi, which Maxie gave to me, and which we decided to donate to charity. Not because we're so virtuous, but because waves of judgment and unpleasantness were wafting off that money like wavy odor lines from a cartoon skunk. We wanted it out of the house. Maxie didn't quite understand that her parents were the ones being criticized, not her—she just knew she felt something shameful. And I felt dirty. I knew I was in the right, but I felt sad and guilty.)

Thankfully, in recent years the tide seems to be turning toward encouraging kids to have more freedom and less micromanagement. (Of course, we're talking about a privileged segment of the population here. There are still plenty of poor families and families of color in which kids are excessively scrutinized or alternatively parents are punished for not having affordable child-care options.)

I need to remind myself sometimes that if one is a human walking this planet, someone, at some point, somewhere, is going to hold up something one does as proof that one sucks at parenting. An illustration: I live across the street from the Hells Angels clubhouse. When Josie was a few months old, I wheeled her out for a walk, and a giant tattooed, bearded man fixing his hog glared at me and yelled, "HE NEEDS A HAT!"

When a Hells Angel informs you that your parenting is substandard, you may be receiving a sign that it's time to stop worrying about other people's judgment. Just saying. I try to remember this story when I sense other people's opprobrium about the way I choose to raise my kids.

## INDEPENDENCE IS AN INOCULATION AGAINST INSULARITY

While anti-Semitism has been a factor in world history ever since the dawn of Jews, there have been periods in which Jews engaged in and enjoyed the wider world. (The Ottoman Empire's sultan mocked Ferdinand and Isabella for expelling the Jews in 1492—what an idiot move on Spain's part! Jews are awesome for the economy. Look how good they are at trade, doctoring, glassblowing, and silk making!) Jews were welcome in the Islamic world in the 1500s and 1600s. Polish cities boasted creative and culturally savvy Jewish populations in the 1700s; in the 1800s German Jews thrived during the Enlightenment era. Those periods of time always brought up questions about "how Jewish" one should be—it's not as though Jews are struggling with questions of identity for the very first time today.

I'd argue that raising kids to be independent, to think for themselves, and to take healthy risks, is vital for living in our modern-day multicultural, diverse world. Getting to know and being able to learn from and work with people who aren't "just like you" is a great pleasure as well as, sadly, a great challenge in contemporary life. Raising kids who are independent means raising kids who are curious about the wider world and eager to explore and see things from different perspectives. Judaism teaches us to stress the importance of asking questions rather than giving answers.

Isidor Isaac Rabi, one of our many Nobel laureates, credited his mother for his accomplishments. (He won a Nobel in 1944 for his discovery of nuclear magnetic resonance—the technology used in MRIs.) Rabi's parents were poor immigrants—his father an unskilled laborer, his mother a housewife in the Lower East Side ghetto—yet he became one of the greatest physicists in history. "My mother made me a scientist," he once said. "Every other Jewish mother in Brooklyn would ask her child after school: 'So? Did you learn anything today?' But not my mother. 'Izzy,' she would say, 'did you ask a good question today?' That difference—asking good questions—made me become a scientist."

For parents, encouraging a child to ask questions and then do his own thinking offers a model for being present and engaged, while urging a child to find his own way. For kids, being encouraged to ask questions means we don't expect a correct answer on the first try, that it's good to look for more data and clarity, that creative and individualistic thinking is more valuable than simply parroting the correct answer. We'll talk more about this in Chapter 6 when we talk about education.

## A HISTORY OF MOTHERLY INDEPENDENCE

Independence is essential for mothers as well as children. To foster your child's independence effectively, you have to be confident in your own. It's difficult to urge kids to be autonomous, unfettered thinkers and doers when you're completely subsuming your own life to theirs. It's also hypocritical: Nurturing kids' selfhood starts with relishing ours. When we make children the raison d'être of our entire lives, we not only stifle their processes of discovery and growth, but also trammel our own. When we make sure to take time for ourselves—through work, volunteering, intellectual and creative or cultural stimulation—we become better parents.

Let's turn for a moment to the *Darmstadt Haggadah,* one of the oldest-surviving guidebooks for the *Pesach* (Passover) Seder. This richly illustrated fifteenth-century traditional text is full of images of women studying. In one scene, men and women sit together around a dinner table, each person holding his or her own haggadah, all animatedly discussing the Exodus from Egypt. This is far from the stereotype of the passive, uneducated Jewish mother of midcentury American myth; emulating historical Jewish motherhood means engaging your own brain, not just fretting about your child's.

Literature and learning have been a source of edification and escape for Jewish women for much of our history. You don't have to be a working mother—though Jewish women frequently were—to have a life apart from your children. Sometimes women's independence came through picking up a book and escaping into another (often child-free) world for a little while.

Back before Gutenberg came up with a mechanical moving-type printing press in the mid-1400s, books were hugely time-consuming and expensive to produce. But a mere hundred years after Gutenberg's invention, there was a vast Yiddish publishing industry throughout Europe. (Yiddish, a heavily Germanic language written with Hebrew characters, originated in central Europe in the ninth century and was the daily language of the Jews; Hebrew was reserved for prayer and ritual texts.) And Jewish women were huge readers.

Booksellers then, like booksellers now, wanted to make money. So they catered to women's tastes. Then, as now, romance was a hugely popular genre. Yiddish publishers churned out epic romances, based on Christian literature, involving knights and jousts and courtly love. One bestselling title was *Bovo-Bukh,* which was first published in 1541 in Venice and went through over forty editions in five centuries. It's essentially fanfic based on a legendary English hero called Bevis of Hampton. (Supposedly the word *bubbemeisa,* which is Yiddish for "old wives' tale" or "grandma legend," actually comes from *Bove-maysa,* or *Bova's Tale,* a bastardization of the name of this romantic epic.) In chivalric romances like Bevis's story, Yiddish writers cut out the most goyish stuff and replaced it with references to Jewish holidays, customs, and traits. Reading, for Jewish women, has long been a source of fun as well as spirituality and self-improvement. And again, it's an indication that counter to stereotype, we had intellectual and emotional lives independent of our children. "Me time" is vital.

Reading hasn't been our only source of escape and self-development, of course. We've had our athletes and entrepreneurs, too.

## ANNIE LONDONDERRY, THE "NEW WOMAN"

I'm kind of obsessed with Annie Londonderry. (Someone turn her story into a children's book!) Like my own grandmother, she was born in Riga, Latvia, and emigrated to Boston as a child. Back then, she was Annie Cohen. By the time she was seventeen, both her parents were dead, and she and her older brother helped raise their younger siblings. In 1888, at eighteen, she married a peddler, became Annie Kopchovsky, and quickly began having children of her own. She helped support her young family by selling newspaper ad space. As legend had it, she overheard a bet one day between two rich men about whether a woman was capable of riding a bicycle around the world. She'd never even *been* on a bicycle, and her kids were only five, three, and two, but she decided she was just the woman for the job.

She found herself a sponsor—Londonderry Lithia Spring Water of New Hampshire—and rebranded herself Annie Londonderry. (Less Jewish, more jaunty!) She made it from Boston to NYC in only eight days, but it took her two months to get to Chicago. When she finally arrived, she ditched her skirt for still-scandalous bloomers, swapped her unwieldy forty-two-pound ladies' bicycle for a much lighter men's version, and resumed her journey. She courted news-papers everywhere she went, sold souvenirs, gave bicycling clinics for women. She "turned herself into a mobile bill-board," wrote her great-great-grandnephew Peter Zheutlin: "Sometimes she was practically covered from head to toe with ribbons, banners, and streamers stitched or attached to her clothing." You know, like racers today.

She did make it around the world, but did so mostly by boat, theatrically taking short land rides on her bike. She became a media darling, a spokeswoman for a bicycle company, and a writer whose account of her journey ran on the front page of the *New York World* newspaper in 1895. She parlayed that into a stunt-reporting job with the *World,* doing a column called "The New Woman." "I am a jour-nalist and 'a new woman,'" she wrote, "if that term means that I believe I can do anything that any man can do."

She hit the lecture circuit, spinning tales of her adventures in India (tiger hunting with German royalty! mistaken for a demon!), Japan (fell through a frozen river! took a bullet! did a stint in prison!), and Siberia ("observed the workings of the Russian system of treating political prisoners," scary!). As you might imagine, she held audiences spellbound. "She has a degree of self-assurance somewhat unusual to her sex," the *San Francisco Chronicle* reported. Her nephew, Zheutlin, wrote a delightful book about her. In doing so, he learned that she'd played a little fast and loose with the truth. She probably made up the story about the bet between rich guys to get publicity for her quest. At various times she claimed to be a lawyer, an heiress, an inventor, a Harvard medical school student, and a senator's niece.

You could argue that Londonderry was a crappy role model; after all, she abandoned her family to go on this quest. She'd kept a kosher home but certainly chucked those standards on the road. On the other hand, she left Boston a poor woman and came home rich enough to buy her family a house in the Bronx. Zheutlin points out that there were only two women athletes who did product endorsements back in 1894: Annie Londonderry and Annie Oakley.

Her story is more than just a fascinating little chapter of athletic and entrepreneurial history. It tells us that there isn't one way to be a Jewish mother. Some of us work outside the home; some don't. There have been times in history in which we've been political and royal insiders, and times in which we've scrabbled in the slums and fled from sword-wielding marauders determined to slice our throats. I'd argue that Londonderry may have taken on her biking challenge to support her family, but she also did it for the adventure. You don't have to be Jewish to appreciate this lesson: We're entitled to value our own dreams and independence. Does Annie's story make me personally want to hop on a bike and head west? No, because I do not like to move unless I am being chased by Cossacks. But it does make me feel less guilty about yearning for at least a chunk of life apart from my kids.

## BEING A GOOD-ENOUGH MOTHER IS GOOD ENOUGH

Having lives of our own may mean we won't be there to wipe away every tear. (I remember when Josie was two and her babysitter painted her nails for the first time. Josie was thrilled, poking her stubby little fingers at me as soon as I came home from the café where I was writing. I went to my bedroom and cried. I knew I was being ridiculous, but I wanted to be the one who gave Josie her first manicure.)

But look, our lives and circumstances vary, and we do our best while frequently feeling our best is not great; and we feel ambivalent whether we work outside the home full-time, part-time, or not at all. This may sound astonishing from a Jewish mother, but I suggest we lose the guilt.

Consider the theories of the British child psychoanalyst Donald Winnicott (1896–1971), the guy who gave us the term "transitional object" (a.k.a. lovey, blankie, or in my daughter Maxie's case, creepy faded gray stuffed elf baby). Winnicott is perhaps best known for coming up with the idea of the "good-enough mother." In 1953, he wrote, "The way to be a good mother is to be a good enough mother." You do your best, but you're allowed to be flawed and sometimes resentful. You get to lose your temper and then yank yourself back from the brink. By being flawed yourself, and acknowledging your own flawed nature, you teach your kid that he or she doesn't have to be perfect. You give a kid the freedom to define his own intellectual interests and goals without getting it all twisted up in pleasing you.

The good-enough mother meets her baby's needs, but also, gradually, lets time lapse between when the baby makes a demand and when the mother fulfills it. That way, as the baby grows up, he learns the difference between self and other, understands that he's not omnipotent, learns to problem-solve for himself. The "perfect" mother, on the other hand, satisfies her child's every need instantly. This mother gets tethered to her kid, unable to have any sort of life of her own, and feels resentful and bullied. The baby never learns to self-soothe or problem-solve and becomes dependent on Mommy to fix all his or her problems.

Bruno Bettelheim (1903–1990) took Winnicott's notion of "good-enough" a step further. Bettelheim's reputation has taken a major hit in recent years—he believed that icy "refrigerator mothers" caused autism, a theory that's been thoroughly discredited, and he was accused of corporal punishment, sexual misconduct, and fabricating some of his credentials—but the guy also had some brilliant ideas about imagination, creativity, and children's emotional resilience. In his book *The Good Enough Parent*, he pointed out that if we grimly persist in trying to model perfection for our children, we teach them that we expect them to be perfect, too.

When we helicopter-parent, we not only don't teach our children independence, we teach them that they're doomed to fail—or at least fall short. Because they quickly learn that in the real world, which shockingly does not, in fact, revolve around them, they won't be repeatedly told they're perfect. We teach them to be cynical (because we've lied to them) and contemptuous of themselves and others (because no one can live up to the impossible standard that's been set for them).

Bettelheim writes, "The goal in raising one's child is to enable him, first, to discover who he wants to be, and then to become a person who can be satisfied with himself and his way of life. Eventually he ought to be able to do in his life whatever seems important, desirable, and worthwhile to him to do; to develop relations with other people that are constructive, satisfying, mutually enriching; and to bear up well under the stresses and hardships he will unavoidably encounter during his life." (Good stuff. Almost good enough to forgive him that refrigerator mother business.)

True independence, for parents and children, is about finding a middle place in which you're neither a slacker nor someone who's so hard-driving she's twisted in knots. It's about not being too hard on yourself, but also not too quick to forgive your own trespasses. The balance between work and family is never static; it shifts one way and the other at different times in our lives. There are times when we yearn for more autonomy and less kid time, and times we yearn to be with the kids more than we are. Work-life balance is an impossible ideal.

## IGNORE CULTURAL MESSAGES TELLING YOU YOU'RE DOING EVERYTHING WRONG

The world is constantly telling us we're doing parenting wrong, no matter how we're doing it. It doesn't help that our flesh-and-blood children refuse to be awesome all the time. There are occasions when, say, one's older child accidentally sets off the burglar alarm when one is not home and completely loses it and calls one screaming and sobbing and hanging up and calling again and sobbing some more, paralyzed with nonsensical terror at the noise and unable to PUSH THE DAMN BUTTONS TO TURN IT OFF, no matter how many times one calmly repeats the code to her. Hypothetically speaking. There are other hypothetical occasions when, say, one's younger child spent about a year of her toddlerhood smacking her older sister as hard as she could, then ran away yelling *"I'm only a baby!"* And of course, she had no idea what she was doing, sarcastically speaking.

In Western culture, no matter what your faith or perspective, you're set up to worry that you're failing all the time. (Marie Wilson, founder of the White House Project, once noted, "Show me a woman without guilt, and I'll show you a man.") You're supposed to have a life of your own but be present at every dentist appointment and school play (but then not brag about it). You're supposed to look gorgeous and put-together and skinny (but you're not supposed to be vain or try too hard). You're supposed to be nurturing (without ever descending into smothering territory). Perpetual perfect is impossible. "Good enough" is more than good enough.

## BUILDING AN INDEPENDENT KID

What choices can we make that ultimately make a kid kind, independent, ethical, hardworking, creative, and engaged in the world? What choices have Jewish mothers made throughout time that have made their kids into successful people who are also not jerkfaces?

Fostering children's independence means letting them learn through doing, which often means learning through mistakes. It means allowing some risk. The old Yiddish saying is true: "If you lie on the ground, you can't fall." But if you're perpetually lying on the ground, you'll never ascend to the heights.

Letting kids be independent sometimes means they will fail. An example: I want my kids to learn to cook. (Because, hey, less work for me.) If I micromanage them in the kitchen, I will be the one at the sauté pan for the rest of my days. And although my children can be lazy—Josie will choose to leave the house hungry rather than make her own eggs, though she knows how—they get furious when I insert myself in their work. Recently they were making a recipe for microwave chocolate-peanut-butter brownies that they'd learned at camp. I desperately wanted to stay in the kitchen, but when I do, I take over. I know this about myself. So I went upstairs. I could hear adorable sisterly chatter, mixing, clattering of spoons. Then I heard a tentative, "Mom?" I came back downstairs. They had tried to melt the chocolate in a cheap little plastic bowl from IKEA. The chocolate and the plastic had elected to become one, in a Zen but foul-smelling and toxic manner. This gave me a chance to explain that no, not all plastic can go in the microwave, and no, they could not scrape some of the chocolate out of the little plastic bowl and eat it. Because it is TOXIC, that's why. Clean the kitchen up, open a freaking window, and oh, by the way, here's how you turn on the stovetop ventilation hood since the kitchen smells like an explosion in a Barbie factory. Yet I'm glad I left them alone to fail, because this is how you learn not to melt things in the wee plastic IKEA bowls.

Independence isn't an either-or, sink-or-swim deal. It's a process. The good-enough parent's way through it is to help a kid along in the process while allowing their child to have the autonomy to blow it now and then.

The ultimate goal of fostering kids' independence is to make sure they have satisfying lives without us. We want them to learn what they love to do, to see what they're capable of, and to separate their own wishes and dreams from ours. The overly authoritarian parent (think Tiger Mom stereotype) makes decisions for her kids and pushes them into existing slots she's chosen for them. Authoritative, rather than authoritarian, parenting (historically, Jewish mothering) is about discovering what your kid's strengths and weaknesses are, letting those passions direct your noodging, and encouraging that kid to grow on their own. As clinical psychologist Jennifer Kunst once wrote, "Winnicott's good enough mother is not so much a goddess; she is a gardener."

## 𝒪𝒪 Mamaleh Methodology

1. What to say to people who disagree with your philosophy of instilling independence, and tell you so: "Thanks for your input, but this works for our family!" There's no way to argue with people who are positive you're doing things wrong. Perhaps you've heard Robert Heinlein's aphorism "Never try to teach a pig to sing—it wastes your time and annoys the pig."

2. **Common sense is your friend.** At thirteen, Josie took the crosstown bus back from a friend's Bar Mitzvah party. She had her phone, her MetroCard, and cash. She called from the crosstown bus stop at 10:30, saying it was a nice night and she wanted to walk the final 10 blocks home. I said I thought it wasn't a good idea and told her the truth: "It's the East Village, it's Saturday night, there are drunk jerks everywhere, and you're alone. I don't think anyone's going to attack you. But a lurching frat boy could leer disgustingly at you or throw up on your shoes. Please take the bus or a cab." She did.

3. **Establish independence-building skills early.** A three-year-old can get their own breakfast cereal and put their bowl in the sink afterward. An eight-year-old can go on short errands for you in the neighborhood. Insist that kids of all ages take a first crack at their homework without any assistance from you. Let your kid learn consequences (even when every fiber of your being wants to intercede and FIX THINGS), which will instill a sense of their own competence when they succeed on their own.

4. **Let your kid fail.** If they always forget their lunch, remind them once, then stop. If they leave it on the counter again, no lunch. Let them live with penalties and deal with consequences. If they don't do their homework, don't write an excuse-filled note. Provide the tools your kid needs to succeed—books, encouragement, role modeling—then, as Elsa says in *Frozen,* let it go.

## Chapter 3

# Maintain Discipline

Do not threaten a child. Either punish him or forgive him.

—*The Talmud*

The goal of discipline is to teach a kid to listen to their own internal voice about right and wrong. You want them to become a moral person, not a person who merely worries about getting caught. In Judaism we talk about the *yetzer hatov* and the *yetzer hara*—the good impulse and the evil impulse, which we all have inside us. It's normal to want to do bad, because bad is often superfun. But part of our job as parents is teaching kids to listen to the *yetzer hatov*, even if the payoff for doing so comes a little later than the instantaneous high we get from listening to the *yetzer hara*.

The Hebrew word for sin is *chet*, which is literally an archery term for "missing the mark." Discipline is a learned skill—like archery—in which practice helps us get closer and closer to the bull's-eye. There's a story about the German Jewish theologian Franz Rosenzweig: When he was asked if he did certain *mitzvot* (commandments, the plural of "mitzvah"), he never answered no. He always said, "Not yet." And he was a theologian! The lesson here is that we're all capable of growing and changing. Our kids don't mean to miss the mark; they're still learning. And so are we. The Jewish tradition expects that learning will be a lifelong process. (The word *Torah*—the central text of Judaism, the five books of Moses—actually comes from a root meaning "to teach" or "to guide." Not coincidentally, it also shares a root with the word for parent, *horeh*. Anyone who tells you Torah means "law" is wrong and you should feel free to correct them, superciliously.)

## THE FIRST TEST OF DISCIPLINE (PREPARE TO SOB UNCONTROLLABLY)

The earliest discipline any parent is expected to impose is sleep training. Guess what? I was a huge failure! Baby Josie's will was way stronger than mine. She could scream for four hours straight, vomit, then scream some more. We tried all the gentle advice books and methods, but tactics like gradually moving your chair out of the room and systematically increasing the time between visits and back pats only made her bellow louder when we left. A couple of weeks into sleep training, I was ready to confess to any nearby supervillain what the nuclear codes were.

At least I had a comrade in arms in the form of my college friend Caroline Bicks, now a Boston College English professor (and the author of *Shakespeare, Not Stirred,* a book of Bard-inspired cocktails that wasn't published until after

I'd finally sleep-trained Josie, which is annoying because I would have drunk my way through the entire book). Caroline's own daughter did not sleep through the night for four years. We all know that whenever other parents ask, all fake solicitous, "Is she sleeping through the night?," they're asking a loaded question. That other parent either wants to lord it over you with her superior-sleeping child and sparkly well-restedness, or seeks reassurance that you suck at parenting as much as she does. Regardless, no one feels sorry for the underrested parent. Everyone's either disgusted with you for your weakness or full of condescending pity for you about your lack of discipline. As Caroline wrote, back in the day: "They just look at you like you represent everything that's wrong with the world: negligence, sloth, incompetence. Like I can't be bothered with sleep training because I'm too busy surfing the Internet for cheap deals on recalled car seats." (Caroline wound up making an appointment with Richard Ferber himself, while fantasizing about him being unable to help, because her baby was *simply too powerful* for even the best sleep doctor in all the land—a medical anomaly, a true outlier! She imagined whipping out a laminated copy of Dr. Ferber's article in the *New England Journal of Medicine* about this brilliant unsleeping baby every time someone patronizingly said, "Have you tried Ferberizing?" But as it happened, during the six months Caroline had to wait for an appointment, the baby learned to sleep on her own. Not perfectly. But well enough.)

Josie did not learn to sleep through the night until my husband initiated full-on Ferberizing while I sat in the living room sobbing and guzzling sauvignon blanc. Eventually the Ferberizing took, though we had several bouts of her refusing to sleep again at ages four, six, and eight, because she was imaginative and easily terrified. After she read Roald Dahl's *The Witches*, she barely slept for four days. When she was eight and we were talking about how creepy the vintage Madame Alexander dolls in Nana's house were, I told her about the "Talky Tina" episode of *The Twilight Zone*. The one with the murderous doll. Welcome to another four days of nighttime fretting and sobbing. But I was an idiot and I *deserved* not to sleep for that.

Thankfully, Maxie was much easier to sleep-train. She's a more easygoing sort than her big sis; they each have their charms and annoying traits, like all of us. Once both girls started sharing a room, Josie could simply climb into Maxie's bed whenever she got scared (this is why you should have two children) and everything worked out okay. Except that now Josie wants to sleep in her own bed and Maxie doesn't want her to. Good times.

Where was I? Oh yes. Discipline is hard. You will frequently be criticized for how you do it no matter what you do. If you let your kid have a tantrum in the supermarket, you will get the side-eye, and if you drag your kid out of the supermarket because your kid is having a tantrum, you will get the side-eye. Fortunately, discipline is not about looking good to other people.

## WHY DISCIPLINE IS VITAL

There's a *midrash* (a story based on Torah teachings) in a tenth-century book called *Tana D'Vei Eliyahu*, about a man who takes his son to synagogue. When the congregation lets out a "Hallelujah," the man's son unleashes some "flippant words." "Look," the people said to the man, "your son is responding with flippant words!" The man replies, "What am I to do with him? He is only a child! Let him amuse himself." The next day, the same thing: Congregation says "Hallelujah," kid responds with flippant words, congregation points out the bad behavior, dad shrugs it off. For the entire festival of *Sukkot* (the eight-day harvest holiday), the son kept mouthing off and the father kept doing nothing to stop him. And then what happened? "Not one year passed by, nor two, nor three, but that the man died, his wife died, his son died, his grandson died, and altogether fifteen souls departed from his house. Only two sons were left, one lame and blind, the other half-witted and malicious."

See what happens when you fail to discipline your child? Your life becomes a Wes Craven movie.

This little story is actually a perfect illustration of the challenges and many meanings of discipline. "Discipline" means both correcting misbehavior and conveying expectations for good behavior. This father excused his kid's rudeness and failed to show the kid alternatives. But discipline has a third meaning, too: It means self-regulation, self-discipline, self-government. It isn't something impressed upon you by an authority figure; it's something that comes from within, something you tap into when you're trying to achieve a goal. Becoming a great scientist, athlete, musician, artist, or lawyer requires discipline. If a kid's going to reach their dreams, our job as parents is to teach them that they alone have to take responsibility. That is what the Jews have been really good at over the years. That is a big part of why our kids have gone on to be so successful, in so many different fields, despite the huge barriers placed in their way. Discipline.

For three decades, psychologist Deborah Baumrind has studied different parenting styles. She uses the descriptor "authoritative parents" for the kinds of parents who are warm but firm. Authoritative parents are happy to discuss and debate things with their kids, but everyone in the house knows that the parent is the ultimate authority. "Authoritarian parents," on the other hand, are supercontrolling and prone to "because I said so, that's why." As a result their kids can become either rebellious or overly dependent on them. And finally, "permissive parents" are warm but not controlling at all; they don't make demands on their kids. As a result, the kid may become an egocentric little *vontz* (Yiddish for bedbug, an excellent term for an annoying person). Apparently there are also "uninvolved parents," but if you're reading this book, guess what—you're not one. Baumrind's research shows that kids do best when parents have high expectations for their behavior, but also provide support when needed, so that kids learn self-control and maintain self-motivation. Those awesome parents are the authoritative parents, also known as The Jews.

I'm kind of over everyone talking about the Marshmallow Test at this point, but even so, it's important, so I'll sum up quickly: A series of Stanford studies by psychologist Walter Mischel involved tiny kids who were told that if they could resist eating a marshmallow for a few minutes, they would then get *two* marshmallows. The kids who were able to wait for the bigger reward were more likely to do better in school and have better life outcomes. These kids had all kinds of strategies, many adorable, for preventing marshmallow-gobbling. They gave themselves pep talks, resolutely looked away from the marshmallow, sang self-distracting songs, told themselves the marshmallow was poison. Discipline is about teaching a kid to avoid temptation and wait and work toward better rewards. But an underreported part of all the reporting on Mischel's marshmallow research has been that if kids don't have a reason to *trust* that they will get the promised second marshmallow—if they've been lied to by researchers in the recent past, for instance, or have learned through hard experience at a very young age that adults are untrustworthy—they're way more likely to go for the instant gratification of the sure-thing single marshmallow.

If you want your kid to develop the self-discipline to navigate the world, your kids have to believe that you'll do what you say. Proverbs 22:6 says, "Train up a child in the way he should go, and even when he is old he will not depart from it." That means follow through on consequences— good and bad—and don't lie to your kids.

Having expectations for your kids and following through on consequences means playing a long game. Research by Sarah E. Hampson, Ph.D., of the University of Surrey in the United Kingdom and the Oregon Research Institute in the United States, has found that children's conscientiousness has a huge positive impact on their well-being as adults: It affects their health, friendships, and accomplishments. In teaching kids discipline and self-control, you're setting them up for life. Because it turns out that being conscientious as a child is a better predictor of adult success and feelings of well-being than being happy as a child.

Childhood happiness is evanescent. Yes, we want our kids to be happy, but we also want them to have the tools to *make themselves happy* in the future, without us . . . and that means giving them a sense of agency. We want them to have self-control and to work hard, which means instilling good discipline now, which will bring joy in the long run. Hampson looked at a variety of different studies and found that kids who weren't conscientious wound up less likely to achieve scholastic and career success and more likely to engage in risky adult behaviors. There are even studies showing that conscientious behavior may mitigate the effects of stress and anxiety. Conscientious people are intrinsically self-motivated: They do their best because it makes them feel good about themselves, not because they're performing like trained seals for a cracker.

Look, I understand why it's tempting to avoid discipline, to cut kids slack, to refuse to say no. Since many of us are working moms, already we feel we have so little time with our families. That makes us conflict-averse, which increases the temptation to try to be friends with our kids. It's our job, though, to be parents, not coconspirators. You *can* be loving and fun without being a pushover.

## ESTABLISH AND MAINTAIN EXPECTATIONS

The term for Jewish law is *halakha*. It literally means "how to walk." Judaism is all about "deed over creed"—actions are more important than beliefs. We are all about walking the walk. This means you have to model behavior for kids rather than just lecturing them about it. Make sure there are meaningful consequences when they don't keep promises or don't behave respectfully or kindly. Talk about your own struggles with discipline—understanding a challenging book, exercising twice a week, taking Spanish lessons, leading a project to completion at work, avoiding snapping at the person in front of you in the checkout line who is putting items on the conveyor belt veeeeeeerrry sloooowwly.

I remember when I was very little, Jimmy Carter was criticized for saying he'd felt lust for women other than his wife. "I've committed adultery in my heart many times," he told *Playboy* magazine. (Advice for future presidents: Do not talk to *Playboy*.) I asked what the man on the TV news was talking about, and my mom explained that people thought the president shouldn't have said what he said. But she also noted in our tradition that we understand people have feelings they might not be proud of. That's the *yetzer hara*. President Carter hadn't actually done anything bad. But in his religion, even having the *feelings* is a sin. For us, on the other hand, not acting on hurtful thoughts is what matters. The very word *halakha* tells you that the doing is what we think is important. Deed over creed.

In the Jewish faith, kids under twelve or thirteen aren't expected to behave like adults, but they're supposed to be responsible from an early age. "A small child who no longer needs his mother's constant attention is required to sit in the sukkah," says one law. (The sukkah is the little temporary shelter we eat and even sleep in during *Sukkot*—it's a sweet wooden or canvas booth in the yard with a roof of boughs through which we can gaze at the stars.) "If a small child is capable of shaking the *lulav* [the ritual palm fronds that are jiggled as part of the Sukkot celebration—as I type this, I realize it sounds insane] correctly, his father should buy him one," another commentator says. Rabbi Nachman of Bratslav (1772–1810), one of Judaism's great sages, said: "At age nine or ten a child should be conditioned to fast during fast days for a limited part of the day." Fasting is tough and requires discipline. (It also requires a discussion about why Jews fast. It's not about dieting; it's about experiencing a bit of discomfort so you think about important historical and communal issues that are more significant than one's own body.)

All these dicta are about establishing expectations for conduct. You make a child feel taken seriously and important when you convey that you think they're capable. You lay a foundation for self-discipline and self-confidence that will sustain the child for their entire life. In trusting them and encouraging them to behave like adults, you say, "I know you can step up." (This is also why, as we discussed in the last chapter, you have to let the child experience consequences if they do fail.)

My mom (whom my brother and I like to call an Important Jewish Educator, overarticulating these words and pronouncing them in exceedingly civilized, slightly British accents, because she actually *is* a brilliant professor of Jewish education and we enjoy mocking her) (she asked me to remove the word *brilliant* and I refused because SHE IS NOT THE BOSS OF ME) pointed out that the Hebrew word for "freedom," *herut,* is connected to the Hebrew word for "carved or etched in stone," *kharoot.* Like the Ten Commandments. Mom said that this ties into the notion that people naturally need restrictions. Freedom without discipline is as destructive as discipline without freedom. Discipline without freedom is the Third Reich; freedom without discipline is *Lord of the Flies.*

We want to build kids who can judge their own capabilities and limits, and who focus on goals without getting discouraged. It's natural for kids to run up against obstacles. We all do. But we want our kids to be willing to try again. (Note: This is what *science* is. Repeating processes to get predictable results. Jews have historically been good at science.)

University of Pennsylvania psychology professor Angela Duckworth, a MacArthur Fellow and "genius grant" winner, studies what she calls "grit," or resilience. People with grit do better in school, tend to earn more, save more, and feel happier about their lives than people who aren't as "gritty." Grit is closely tied to discipline, in that it means having self-command and being flexible, strong, quick to recover from setbacks, determined to crash through barriers. (I do want to note that grit alone isn't enough to succeed—you have to have education, social support, a safety net. And it shouldn't be a justification for eliminating assistance for less privileged kids.)

## AVOIDING HAVING TO DISCIPLINE IN THE FIRST PLACE

The easiest way to discipline your kid is to avoid situations where you have to bring out the heavy artillery. Easy example: Don't shop when your kid is hungry. Promise your kid one thing in the checkout line, and keep reminding him what is going to happen. Have a nice, distracting conversation as you shop. Ask for the kid to point out the things you're looking for that you somehow cannot see even though they are directly in front of you. Debate the prettiest produce. Keep the kid engaged and ask for their input so you head off tantrums before they're even a glimmer in your child's eye. You get the idea.

For many years, the big discipline challenge with Maxie

was that she started becoming a werewolf at 7 p.m. My sweet, funny, agreeable child would turn contrary, insane, and pointy fanged. It wasn't until she was almost six that I figured out we had to get everything done before 7 p.m., and then all was well. (Duh.) An actual conversation with her, two months before her sixth birthday, at 7:05 p.m.:

ME: Max, please go get your bathing suit and put it in your backpack for tomorrow.

MAXIE: You do it. I am exhausted.

ME: Excuse me? This is your job. We can rest and cuddle and read after you get your bathing suit.

MAXIE: FINE. I will do it this ONE TIME but NEVER AGAIN! I cannot continue to do EVERYTHING around here!

She got her suit. Did I say "Do not speak to me in that tone of voice?" I did not. She did what I wanted her to do; that was good enough. (Please see "Is this the hill you want to die on?" at the end of this chapter.) Eventually I figured out that I had to ask her to pack her backpack for the next day before dinner, not after. What I do *not* do is pack her backpack for her. Even though that would be a lot quicker. Independence + Discipline = Successful Grown up.

The most effective discipline takes into account a kid's feelings and tendencies. Does a kid act out when they're hungry? Do they get claustrophobic when other kids are too close? Are they good at art, leadership, math, imaginative play—things you can encourage them with when they're bummed about not being so good at other things? When Max was younger, she was easily distracted, and her kindergarten teacher told me about research showing that chewing gum helped kids focus. And indeed, it kept her from tuning out and from sprawling all over the place and annoying other kids, which kept the teacher from having to discipline her. Preventive awesomeness. But in Hebrew school, a teacher who didn't know about this research once berated and shamed her publicly for chewing gum in class. When Maxie came home crying, I Googled a bunch of the research and gave it to the teacher. I didn't yell at her, and I didn't pull Maxie from her class. (Look how disciplined I was.)

In general, studies have found that trying to control kids' behavior—rather than helping them learn to control it themselves—short-circuits their ability to develop a sense of their own competence and autonomy. It destroys their motivation to do better for *their own sake* and turns being good into a performance for others, not a choice they make for their own moral development.

A key concept in Jewish tradition is *derech eretz*. It means respect and common courtesy. We show our kids we respect them, and they offer us respect back. *Derech eretz* literally means "the way of the land" (yeah, we *wish*). Treating others with dignity and humanity is essential in Jewish life. (I'm perpetually amused when commenters on my articles who are far to the right of me politically accuse me of terrible parenting, Jewish self-hatred, hating Israel, and causing the Holocaust. Calling others nasty names on the Internet is not *derech eretz*.)

## RESPECT IS A TWO-WAY STREET

Respect for parents is a pretty big deal in the Torah—it's one of the *Ten Commandments*. But we can't expect respect as our due automatically. *Pirkei Avot,* which means "Ethics of the Fathers"—part of Jewish oral law that was first compiled in the second century CE, do try to keep up—says, "Who is honored? The person who honors others."

Need I point out that trying to beat a kid into respect doesn't work as a disciplinary strategy? As Talmud *Baba Batra* puts it, "If you strike a child, strike them only with a shoelace." (But don't wing it toward their face.) Hitting someone is not a way to show regard. That said, I have swatted a kid's butt once or twice in a fury. Then I've regretted it and discussed it later with the swattee. No children were harmed in the making of this book.

Hitting is not courteous, but neither is being churlish in one's speech. Model the behavior you want to see. As my friend Carla Naumberg, Ph.D., noted in an article about mindful parenting, "Some of us may have heard of the prohibition against *lashon hara,* which tends to be commonly translated as 'gossip.' However, the phrase *sh'mirat ha'lashon,* or 'guarding the tongue,' may offer additional guidance to parents trying to figure out the most empathic and effective ways to speak with, and to, their children."

This means being careful about what you say, not just avoiding gossip. It means saying kind things about other people when your kids can overhear. It means not being snarky to your spouse on the phone even when he didn't put his dinner meeting in the calendar and you were waiting for him to get home before you gave the kids dinner and everyone is starving and whining and he's not answering his texts. It means not saying cruel things about other people's bodies, or even about your own. There's a 1950s joke about a kid who tells his mom he knows what an *alta kocker* is. (It's Yiddish for a doddering elderly person; literally it means "old shit.") The mom says hesitantly, "What do you think it means?" The kid says, "A slow driver!"

Another kind of respect we can offer our kids is respect for their private space (not reading their diaries, knocking before you enter the bathroom) and respecting their own strategies for getting their work done. (We've tried to create comfortable workspaces for the kids at desks in their room and at the dining room table; they want to work at the kitchen counter.) My husband's doctorate is in communication theory and research, and his great interest is privacy, so our kids have had an earful about not giving away too much information online. Both my kids text like fiends, and the older one has a Tumblr blog (a mix of pop culture and intersectional feminist rants), and we're pretty confident in their ability to manage social media. You have to give kids tools to make choices.

They will likely screw up. We all do. The challenge then becomes "How do we make things right?" I will never, ever forget the time I literally hissed in Josie's face when she was three, "YOU ARE MAKING MY LIFE HARDER INSTEAD OF EASIER. ARE YOU HAPPY ABOUT THAT?" The words were bad, but my face was worse. I was furious, and my voice was really low and lethal, and I'd put my face right up into hers. Josie's little face scrunched up, and silent tears rolled down her chubby little cheeks, and I felt absolutely sick with self-loathing. That was a failure of discipline on my part; I lost control. Later, I apologized, and she accepted, but I've never forgotten that queasy, awful feeling.

Now that my kids are older, they understand that both their parents have tempers. They know we try our best to control our words and sometimes fail. (True of Josie, too. Maxie is inexplicably even-keeled.) When my girls were little, both loved a picture book called *Harriet, You'll Drive Me Wild!* by Mem Fox. It's about a kid who just keeps screwing up, on purpose or not—knocking over her juice, getting paint all over the rug, sliding off her chair at the table and taking the tablecloth with her. When the mom in the book finally loses it, she loses it spectacularly, yelling and yelling and yelling. Harriet cries. But then the mom pulls herself together and apologizes and the two hug it out and clean up the mess together. It's an adorable book, but one that makes the very real point that none of us is perfect. Moms can explode now and then, but they still love their kids. We're only human, and that's good enough. (I should probably add, though, that if you feel out of control or depressed about your parenting failures a lot of the time, you might want to seek professional help. Doing so is a sign of strength, not weakness.)

When Josie was three and we were visiting my mother-in-law in Milwaukee, we were all invited to a lovely engagement party at the home of my mother-in-law's friends. All the kids were sent to play in their big suburban basement. Josie kept coming upstairs to report that two older boys, around five and seven, were teasing her, calling her a baby, saying they were going to knock over her blocks, threatening to make her clean their rooms. She kept asking us for more solutions. (She was stunned when their response to "If you're not nice to me, I won't be your friend," was "We don't WANT to be your friend!" It was so not in her pre-schooler's playbook, in which being told you can't be some-one's friend was the *worst* thing you could possibly threaten.) My husband told her "Ignore them. Just walk away." This did not occur. I don't know what the final straw was, but suddenly Josie was chasing the two older boys through the house with an oversized wiffle bat, roaring, before nailing one in the balls.

We talked afterward about strategies to control our temper and how no matter what someone says we don't hit. But I must also admit I was secretly pleased. Those boys were truly assholes. Later, I listened in as she reported the story to my mother on the phone. "Daddy says that when someone teases me, I should walk away. And I did walk away. But then I came back. With a bat." The fact that I did not burst out laughing is to my endless parenting credit, don't you think?

Discipline means not only controlling one's rage, but also following through on commitments. We don't quit the play even if we didn't get the part we wanted, because peo-ple are relying on us. Your sister may indeed have acciden-tally gotten the bigger half of the cookie, but this is how the cookie crumbled and you do not moan endlessly about it. Everyone else may indeed be going to the party, but we are going to Bubbe's for dinner. Life isn't fair.

These days, I don't punish all that often. But I do talk about my feelings of disappointment: in myself, in them, in elected officials, in the news, in celebrities, in books. (Being disappointed is the Jewish mother way.) There are so many teachable moments that inform your kid about your belief in the importance of discipline, in choosing one's words and actions and not being lazy. For example, I point out the laziness of comedians who make fun of politicians' weight or looks when there are so many substantive things to mock them about. I talk about why I'm angry at myself for not finishing a project on deadline (hello, book that is a year late) or forgetting to do something I'd promised my husband I'd do. Not long ago, Josie told me she was disappointed in me when she felt I was pressuring her to opt out of a standardized test she wanted to take. Conversations about discipline become meta-conversations as children age: What are the expectations for a civilized society? How do we do the thing that may not be easy, but is right?

## MAKE AMENDS WHEN YOU CAUSE HURT

Our wonderful babysitter Rita told me this story: When Maxie was four, Rita was giving her a bath and said something teasing to her, and Maxie snapped "Shut up!" The moment the words were out of her mouth, Maxie blanched. She said, "I'm sorry! Sometimes words pop into my brain and then they have to come out my mouth or I feel like I'm swallowing flies."

That's a good way to describe the feeling of knowing immediately that you've said something dreadful. What's harder is having the courage to say you're sorry afterward. It's tempting to pretend your failing never happened, but that's a cop-out. Judaism is big on apologies. The High Holidays—Rosh Hashanah and Yom Kippur—are all about repentance and making amends. They're not just about saying you're sorry to God for your year of misdeeds; you have to apologize to human beings, too. And you know how earlier we spoke of walking the walk? The Hebrew word for "penitence" also has to do with walking: *Teshuvah.* It literally means return, as in a return to the path you've deviated from. It's important to convey to your kids, when you discipline them, that you believe they haven't truly left the path, that you still love them, that you believe in their ability to right their own wrongs.

For fun, my friend Susan McCarthy and I do a website called SorryWatch, in which we examine apologies in the news, literature, and pop culture. If more parents taught their children to apologize well (and actually mean it) as part of the process of discipline, we could retire the website. There's a reason it's hard for us to find good apologies to spotlight: Apologizing is difficult. You have to be humble; you have to name what you did wrong when you'd really rather forget it or allude to it cryptically; you have to consider the other person's feelings and prize them before your own. A good apology takes a ton of discipline.

I know there are experts who don't believe in making little kids say they're sorry when they don't mean it. I disagree. When kids are very young, I think teaching them how to express the sentiment, and explaining why it is essential, and talking about the hurt caused and the need to be a *mensch,* a good person, ultimately leads to the actual feelings of repentance and regret. Metaphorically speaking, apology—like intelligence and self-control—is a muscle. As kids get older, they can understand more nuance: You may well be the wronged party, but you may choose to apologize for the sake of *shalom bayit* (peace in the house, or by extension in the community or school or friendship).

If you know you're wrong and have done something horrid, you should apologize even though you don't think you'll be forgiven. The twelfth-century Jewish scholar Maimonides said that you have to approach someone three separate times to ask for forgiveness before you can give up. When you're the wronged party, and someone sincerely asks your forgiveness, Maimonides says you're obligated to give it. It can be tempting to seethe, and my children come from a long line of seethers. But Rabbi David Wolpe once wrote, "The grudge perches on the heart like a gargoyle on a parapet." And Buddha (not a Jew) supposedly said, "Holding on to anger is like grasping a hot coal with the intent of throwing it at someone else; you are the one getting burned." (Buddha and David Wolpe should have dinner.)

Stepping up and apologizing well is one of those acts that helps a kid take a leap forward in maturity. That's what we're going for when we discipline our kids: making them internalize the feelings and behaviors that will make them responsible, caring, "gritty," self-regulating grown-ups. It's all too easy for kids to get trapped in their own entitlement and resentments, trapped in relying on their parents for rescue, trapped in parents' seemingly impossible expectations. The Hebrew word for Egypt, where we were slaves for generations, is *Mitzrayim*. Literally the word means "a narrow place." The inability to shore up one's self-discipline and make one's own way in the world is a modern-day narrow place.

Aristotle (not a Jew, but still a mensch) said, "Virtue requires practice." We need to discipline our children—and ourselves—to be good people. We need to expect slipups while continuing to provide opportunities to get it right. Then we make the choice to punish or forgive.

## 𝟞𝟞 Mamaleh Methodology

1. **Plan ahead; avoid situations in which you're likely to yell or punish.** When I think back over most of my kids' meltdowns—the kind where there's no pulling back from the brink, and all you can do is let the kid scream in their room—a lot of them could have been avoided if I'd headed them off at the pass. Some examples: Many little kids, including mine when they were small, have trouble with transitions. So don't spring things on your kid. Get them used to the idea that here's what we're doing today, here's when we're leaving, here's a reminder, here's a warning. Don't sneak out when you drop your kid off at preschool for the first week; give a big hug, say a firm good-bye and I'll see you soon, and get the hell out of Dodge. Creeping out the door like a thief in the night only teaches your child that he can't trust you. Even if he was fine and engaged when you left, if he thinks you betrayed him by leaving him in a strange place, you've made life harder for both of you.

2. **Keep telling yourself that to teach a kid discipline, you need discipline yourself.** If you say something will have a consequence, it needs to have a consequence. If you threaten, you better follow through. If you announce, "We're leaving in ten minutes!" set your watch and *leave in ten minutes.* Whether you offer a threat, a bribe, or a promise, do what you say you'll do. A saying in the Talmud goes, "A parent should not promise to give a child something and then not give it, because in that way the child learns to lie." Be true to your word.

3. **"Is this the hill I want to die on?"** As my kids get older, this is the parenting advice I give myself every day. I imagine life as

a tumbleweed-strewn street in the Old West, and I have a six-shooter and there are threats lurking behind every swinging saloon door (allow me my fantasies; I've seen a lot of movies) and I think: *I have a certain amount of ammunition and no more so I'm not going to waste it on idle threats. I might need these bullets later.* So the question always is: Is this a battle worth fighting? If not, lay down the big guns, take a few breaths, and distract yourself so you can detach yourself.

4. **DO NOT CAVE.** Sometimes I *do* want to die on that hill. I am Shane. And I am going to clean up the town and save it from the ruthless cattle baron and I am noble and my children are psychopathic little Jack Palances. When you've made the choice to have a rule or issue a dictum, do not negotiate with terrorists. Do not wheedle and beg for cooperation and help in the difficult task of parenting. Children do not care how hard it is to parent. That's why you have to make expectations and values clear at all times, and not get all overexplainy and overpraisey and overpsychologizey and wheedley about enforcement. Is the rule "We don't hit"? Then when the kid hits, you do not say, "What did that boy do to make you hit him?" Instead, you announce, "You're done. We're going home." Have few hard-and-fast rules, but stick religiously to the ones you have, rather than going to pieces and flapping your hands helplessly and offering endless warnings and toothless punishments.

5. **Talk about feelings.** Part of what makes kids want to be good is having empathy for others. When you hit or bite, you hurt others. When you use mean words or exclude someone else from play, you cause emotional hurt. How do you get

kids to think about other people's feelings? First, start early to make sure kids have the vocabulary to identify them. When your child is angry, sad, or frustrated, put a name to the feelings, and brainstorm together about how the child could feel better. As your kid gets older, talk to her about your own strategies for maintaining your self-control. Deep breathing helps me. Composing a nasty e-mail and then sending it to myself instead of the intended recipient helps. Taking a walk. Petting the cat. Josie plugs in to her favorite music and sings her heart out; Maxie rereads a favorite funny book.

6. **Work together on conflict resolution strategies.** Your kid is much more likely to wind up getting disciplined at school if he hasn't had practice resolving conflicts at home. You can role-play different responses to a hypothetical fight, or talk about a bad situation you saw in a cartoon or read about in a book and discuss how the problem could have been defused. And if your kid is a perfect angel at school and Beelzebub in your house, I'm sorry and congratulations. You're doing something right. Your kid is releasing pent-up feelings from maintaining control all day; look to methodological strategies one to five for use at home and give yourself a mental high five for raising a kid who "shows well," as they say at the Westminster Kennel Club.

*Chapter 4*

# Distrust Authority

God created a world full of little worlds.

*—Yiddish proverb*

When Josie was six, she regaled me with stories about a badly behaved kid in her class. I told her, "Even if he's a jerk to everyone, I don't want you to be mean to him. I want you to turn the other cheek." She narrowed her eyes. "What if he throws a rock at it?"

Josie, here, is a stand-in for the Jewish people. We have generally expected someone to throw a rock.

To be fair, Jews have had good reasons to be wary of the rabble, as well as of secular political and church leadership, over millennia. The whole *killing us* thing was very unpleasant, and the *expelling us* business was not much better. But Jews have also raised an eyebrow at authority even within our own community. And I'd argue that this skepticism is a big part of why Jews have been so successful.

We are a people who just love dissenting opinions. We also enjoy questioning, yammering, challenging, and disputing. The Talmud, the compendium of Jewish law, is pretty much a bunch of dudes contradicting one another. Each page consists of a big box of text in the middle and wrapped around it like a frame is lots of "Wait, you think *what*?" and "No, Rabbi Akiva, *YOU* shut up!" all in different voices; in smaller text, a torrent of arguing and sword-crossing and horn-locking and pontificating.

This conversational style actually models excellent lessons for kids, one many Jewish parents still use today. Our offspring quickly learn that it's important to pay attention and keep up. As our words gnip gnop around (I just invented a verb), kids don't have time to get bored. In addition, they see us grown-ups blurting out encouragement and showing enthusiasm, which are excellent things for kids to experience. They see that no one perspective automatically holds more weight than any other, as long as you can support your thesis. There's also the fact that valuing verbal quickness and daring can lead to success (and maybe Juilliard and Yale Law School degrees) later in life.

Of course, not everyone loves the way we talk. Linguist Deborah Tannen has written that negative stereotypes of Jews may be grounded in common Jewish linguistic patterns, such as the introduction of new topics into a discussion and persistence in reintroducing topics if others don't immediately pick up on them. Tannen notes that Jews tend to talk more quickly than other ethnic groups, take fewer pauses, interrupt more often, and engage in "high-involvement cooperative overlapping"—that is, talking over someone else without perceiving it as interrupting. (We see it as expressing interest and agreement, and engagement in the conversation. Talking is listening!) This antic style can be irksome to the mellow WASP. Furthermore, a survey of 30,053 American non-Jews and Jews conducted by Sarah Bunin Benor and Steven M. Cohen at Hebrew Union College found that 47 percent of Jews report they have been told some or many times that their speaking style is "too aggressive"—as opposed to 36 percent of non-Jews.

Being mouthy has been a mixed blessing for Jewish women in particular. On the one hand, it has made Jewish men write snotty books and comedy routines about us. But on the other, it has led to menschy, creative, and independent kids. It also means we've often had impressive careers of our own. In *Lean In,* Sheryl Sandberg advocates a lot of the kinds of behaviors that have gotten Jewish women criticized. She writes that women tend to be too self-effacing . . . which isn't exactly something Jewish women are often accused of. She writes that women tend to undercut their career promise by being passive—again, not a common accusation leveled at my people. The whole Cult-of-True-Womanhood-submissive-domesticity thing has never been our shtick. Jewish women have *always* struggled with work-life balance, because throughout history we've often been our family's primary breadwinner. But assertiveness and engagement have served us pretty well over time. They've worked for our progeny, and they can work for us in a world that promises to but doesn't actually reward women for being passive, good girls. Jewish women hardly expect the people who hold the reins of power to simply hand them over to us. History has given us little reason to trust that if we aren't aggressive, we won't get *bupkes*. (That's Yiddish for *nothin'*.)

What does all this mean for you, the modern-day

parent? Take a deep breath. I am about to encourage you to (1) argue with your child and (2) encourage your child to be very wary of the establishment.

## DIVERSITY OF OPINION IS GOOD

There's a saying: Two Jews, three synagogues. It's based on an old joke about a Jew shipwrecked on a desert island for years. When rescuers finally come, they're astonished by the way the man has built a comfortable hut, a water collection and filtration system, an automated coconut peeler, an outhouse. "What are those two buildings over there?" the rescuers ask him. "Oh, that one's my synagogue!" the man says, pointing to the building on the left. "But what's the other building?" the rescuers say. The guy replies, "Oh, that's the synagogue I'd *NEVER SET FOOT IN! Ptui!*"

The joke has a real-life analog: In Rome, in the year 1555, Pope Paul IV decreed that the Jews of the city could have only one synagogue. This was no doubt as horrifying to Jews then as it would be today. We are a people who cannot agree on who has the best pastrami, let alone on how best to worship. So instead of banding together and coming to some sort of theological compromise, the Jews of Rome set up six different areas of worship *within the same synagogue.* That "magnificent fractiousness," in the words of writer Stephen Marche, is essential to who we are. The Jews of Rome treated religious authority like a line of food trucks in Los Angeles. When you don't like what one is serving, you can just move on down the line.

Judaism is a faith that doesn't defer to a single central authority. We have no pope. Rabbi means "teacher," not "leader." We have a number of prayers you aren't even allowed to recite without a *minyan,* a quorum, a minimum number of people. (They include the traditional seven blessings for a wedding couple, the prayer for the dead, the prayer to comfort a mourner, and the reading of the Torah.) There's a Yiddish expression, *"Nayn rabonim kenen keyn minyen nit makhn ober tsen shusters yo."* Nine rabbis can't make a *minyan* but ten shoemakers can. In other words, the presence of community is what's essential, not the authority of a single dominant official or point of view.

By now I think you probably get that Jews, as opposed to some other religious and cultural groups, have always understood that not everyone will come up with the same answer to a given question *why.* Some Orthodox Jews maintain that there's only one way to be Jewish, but if you look at our collective history, it's one of discussion and debate. I'd argue that this attitude—question everything, do your own thinking, put forth an informed opinion, and be willing to expect disagreement as well as be willing to engage with those who disagree—has been essential to Jews' success over the years.

Shoemakers and rabbis alike should have some familiarity with Jewish texts, history, and culture. This means you, the parent, do not need to know everything . . . but you should strive to know something. If you are a person of the tribe whose grounding in Judaism isn't so strong, may I suggest you have a poke around the My Jewish Learning website, watch Simon Schama's *The Story of the Jews,* buy some Klezmatics and Matisyahu albums, go to a Sephardic dance festival, and/or challenge your family to find the best damn hummus recipe in the world. If you are not a Jew, may I propose you explore your own background for sources of pride, information, and values. Once you've gotten a grounding in your own history, it's easier to relax and find your breathing space in it. This is true whatever your religion is: Explore your traditions, and then decide what works for you. Because I am personally a troublemaker, I love hearing about the rebels and authority flouters in other people's traditions. Bring on the rabble-rousing feminist nuns!

We want kids to question existing paradigms, enjoy the process of learning, and understand the value of discussion and debate. That's how they'll develop their own independent skills in how to reason and think and build and experiment, and how they'll cope with the disappointment of sometimes getting it wrong. Our patron saint is Ms. Frizzle from *The Magic School Bus* (or she would be, if we had saints in Judaism)—her motto was "Take chances, make mistakes, get messy!" Remember the words of Nobel-winning scientist Isidor Rabi: "Did you ask a good question today?" Ask your kid questions regularly, and listen to the answers. Don't let them get away with facile reasoning. Gently point out flaws and contradictions in their argument. Talk about the questions you yourself are struggling with, and ask for your kid's opinions. I'm not saying you should respect your child's reasoning that they should not have to go to bed until their forty-eighth game of *Grand Theft Auto* has been completed. I'm saying you should encourage civil debate and urge your kid to view the world with a gimlet eye.

In a piece in *Wired* magazine a few years ago, Joi Ito, the head of the MIT Media Lab (and not a Jew), outlined the skills people need to survive in a rapidly changing world. These skills included being resilient (so you can bend and yield and bounce back from failure), taking risks instead of focusing on safety, relying on compasses instead of maps, nurturing disobedience instead of compliance ("You don't get a Nobel Prize for doing what you are told"), and focusing on learning instead of education. These skills are connected to not trusting blindly in those in charge and to having healthy, intrinsic self-esteem, the kind that comes from learning to trust your internal voice instead of the chorus of nags, drones, and naysayers around you.

## NEVER FORGET THAT THE WORLD IS OUT TO GET YOU

Here's a question for you: Why have Jews been a largely urban bunch of entrepreneurs, bankers, financiers, lawyers, doctors, writers, traders, and scholars? Why are there so few Jewish farmers? Why have we scattered so far and wide across the globe, but somehow wound up in cities, working in creative and scientific and money-related fields?

Because we learned not to trust authority! After we were kicked out of the land of Israel in 70 CE (thanks, Romans), we roamed around for centuries. At various times in history we weren't allowed to own land, were excluded from membership in craft and merchant guilds, and pushed into money lending because Christians weren't allowed to lend money with interest, so hey, opportunity. But a recent book by two economists, one in Israel and one at Princeton, argues that when the Jews figured out they were going to be homeless and Temple-less (because the Romans destroyed the building that was central to our sense of peoplehood), they developed a self-image based on study and literacy.

In *The Chosen Few: How Education Shaped Jewish History 70–1492*, Maristella Botticini and Zvi Eckstein argue that once we Jews had no central Temple to define us, our picture of who we were and what defined us shifted. We reinvented ourselves, from a cult based on ritual sacrifices in specific time and place to a group focused on Torah study and literacy. Basically, decentralization saved us after we lost the physical setting that had made us who we thought we were.

As we roamed the world, we did what we had to do to earn a living while focused on literacy, which became central to our identity. Between 750 and 900 CE, Botticini and Eckstein say, almost all the Jews in Mesopotamia and Persia—nearly 75 percent of world Jewry—left agriculture, moved to the urban centers, and entered skilled occupations. By the 1300s, we'd pretty much blanketed the world, and we were the People of the Book—actually, the people of lots of books.

Back then, much of the world was illiterate. So Jews' ability to read and write contracts and business letters and keep account books gave them an advantage . . . and these skills were portable. After being booted from their homeland, Jews also developed their own code of law (the Talmud) and institutions (rabbinic courts and the *responsa,* a body of written decisions and rulings of Jewish legal scholars) that helped foster community values across many different countries. Knowing that we couldn't count on the places where we lived to protect and defend us, we created a democratic authority structure that crossed country lines and relied on communal ethics.

When you don't know what the future holds, knowledge is the best currency you can have. (Plus when you keep crossing borders, the *actual physical currency* keeps changing.) Your brains—not a given country's political leaders, judicial system, or civic institutions—are reliable constants in an unreliable world. There is a lesson here for you, modern-day parent: Focus on helping your kid develop passions and skills that will last forever; don't focus on transitory grades and test scores. Real knowledge and critical thinking skills will outlast any academic trends or jargon (Common Core, Race to the Top, STEM, smath, who can keep up?).

## BETTER TO SAY "I DON'T KNOW" THAN TO PRETEND YOU DO

Nurturing kids' curiosity is one of the keys to Jewish parenting's success. Curiosity is a healthy driving force in rapidly changing times. Being open to hearing different answers, being able to accept that there may be multiple truths, being accepting of difference in general—all are helpful for success in America, a New World country that values independence and quick thinking over pedigree and tradition.

That's why it's key to teach your kid "process, not product." How you get to the answer is as important as the answer itself. If you're a scientist, you want to be able to achieve reproducible results. If you're an actor, you don't try to deliver a monologue exactly the way some previous performer did, even if that guy won an Oscar. You want to get into your character's head in your own way, put your own stamp on the production. It's totally fine not to be an expert when you embark on something new. I worry that kids today don't want to be beginners, don't want to be imperfect, don't want ever to look clueless. But the Talmud says, "Teach your tongue to say 'I don't know.' " How else will you learn? It's infinitely worse to *pretend* to know. Pretending has a domino effect of worsening self-esteem, cheating in school, an overall sense of imposter syndrome—that you're an empty shell without a soul inside. A pretender. *Feh, feh, feh.* Authority has to be earned, and we should respect those on the way to earning it, without taking shortcuts.

Being wary of authority—and learning how to gain authority legitimately—means not only making sure kids know that they aren't supposed to be immediately great at everything, but also encouraging kids to be supportive of different gifts and abilities and challenges. No one is good at everything. Do not be a jerk to those who are not as accomplished as you, but don't overidolize those who are better. Hard work is as important as talent. Respect the work and the individual doing it.

The best Jewish parenting nurtures both creativity and *chutzpah*. Those qualities are what have made our people succeed in a zillion different environments. Even cultures that generally haven't been big fans of coloring outside the lines acknowledge that we may be onto something: In a recently published memoir, Wu Guanzheng, a former high-ranking Chinese official, reflected on why Jews have been so successful: It's because of our "ability to speak truth to power" and "freely express different opinions." Ironic that a big macher in an authoritarian system thinks our openness and rebelliousness are great, but hey, yay us.

It's essential that adults stop regarding children as empty vessels to be filled with prefab knowledge; instead, the goal should be to turn them into lifelong learners, self-starters, people who find ideas sparky and exciting. And that means encouraging them not to take conventional wisdom for granted. It means living in the whys. Of course you want them to do well in school, but historically it's turned out to be more important for the Jewish people (especially since we weren't always able to go to school, or get degrees in the fields we wanted to) to learn to question and think and argue and defend their points of view. Parroting back what a teacher says may get you an A, but it won't help you approach subjects critically or shatter paradigms.

You never know where wisdom will come from. That's why rather than sticking to canonical texts or traditional fonts of knowledge, it's important to read and explore widely. *Pirke Avot, Ethics of Our Fathers,* says, "Who is wise? One who learns from everyone." Textbooks are only one way to learn, and experiences and fellow students are as important as teachers.

We want our children to explore, to find careers that are personally fulfilling and meaningful to them. We see kids as individuals with different gifts and passions. Unlike the stereotypical Tiger Mother, we encourage kids to dabble in activities, letting them figure out what they really enjoy. We welcome playdates rather than viewing them as distractions from school; we believe that kids learn from peers and need chill-out time. We don't fetishize the teacher as the ruler of the classroom and the font of all knowledge; we encourage kids to be polite in class, but never to stop asking questions and never to sit with answers that don't feel right. (I once had a high school teacher who insisted that the word *manumission* meant "punching someone." He said it came from the Latin root *manu,* meaning "hand," and *missio,* meaning "send": sending out your hand to connect with someone else's face! After I got this wrong on a vocabulary test, I showed him the word in the dictionary, where it was defined as "the act of a slave owner freeing his slaves." The teacher replied, "A word means what I say it means." I did not get credit for my answer on the test. But I retained the lesson that authority figures do not know everything, and that they sometimes use their power unjustly.)

## GETTING OUT OF THE NARROW PLACE

Awareness of injustice is central to Jewish identity and child-rearing. (There's a joke that every Jewish holiday has one narrative: "They tried to kill us, we won, let's eat.") One of the Jews' formative experiences as a tribe is the time we spent as slaves in Egypt. As I mentioned earlier, the word for Egypt in Hebrew is *Mitzrayim*, "narrow place." Egypt was narrow because Jews had no autonomy, no rights, no power. Pharaoh was an unjust ruler. During the Passover Seder, when we commemorate this time and our escape from it, many of us who now live in relative comfort and ease talk about the narrow places in which we currently reside: being afraid to stand up to injustice, failing to be our best selves, not pushing ourselves beyond our own comfort zones.

Today, in many synagogues, we recite "A Prayer for Our Country." It asks God to bless our government and all who exercise just and rightful authority. It hopes that those in power will use insights from the Torah to administer fairly, so that "peace and security, happiness and prosperity, justice and freedom may forever abide in our midst."

The prayer reflects anxiety about unjust authority—it starts with a plea for fair-mindedness, then goes on to hope that citizens of all races, backgrounds, and belief systems will "forge a common bond in true harmony, to banish hatred and bigotry, and to safeguard the ideals and free institutions that are the pride and glory of our country." The prayer acknowledges and welcomes diversity and difference and pleads for people to work together for the betterment of all. It concludes, "May this land, under Your providence, be an influence for good throughout the world, uniting all people in peace and freedom—helping them to fulfill the vision of Your prophet: 'Nation shall not lift up sword against nation, neither shall they learn war any more.'"

What I find so striking about the prayer is its view of the world as decentralized, its implicit statement that leadership is often flawed and unfair, and that uniting people and creating peace requires a collective effort of will. There's suspicion of authority built into the prayer, it seems to me, but also a hope that people collectively will rise to the challenge of unity.

I suspect that the ability to live among others while keeping a sense of self, and to be wary of secular leadership, while fostering a sense of collective identity tied to being decent (and brainy and literate) is key to the Jews doing so well for themselves. In his 1896 essay "Concerning the Jews," Mark Twain wrote, "If the statistics are right, the Jews constitute but one per cent of the human race. It suggests a nebulous dim puff of star-dust lost in the blaze of the Milky Way. Properly the Jew ought hardly to be heard of; but he is heard of, has always been heard of. He is as prominent on the planet as any other people, and his commercial importance is extravagantly out of proportion to the smallness of his bulk. His contributions to the world's list of great names in literature, science, art, music, finance, medicine, and abstruse learning are also away out of proportion to the weakness of his numbers . . . The Egyptian, Babylonian, and the Persian rose, filled the planet with sound and splendor, then faded to dream-stuff and passed away. The Greek and Roman followed, made a vast noise and they are gone. Other peoples have sprung up, and held their torch high for a time, but it burned out and they sit in twilight now or have vanished. The Jew saw them all, beat them all, and is now what he always was, exhibiting no decadence, no infirmities of age, no weakening of his parts, no slowing of his energies, no dulling of his alert and aggressive mind. All things are mortal, but the Jew. All other forces pass, but he remains."

Part of why we've remained is that core sense of self—as distinct from the evanescence of the world around us—that makes us thrive in all kinds of environments and be able to get along with many kinds of people. I grew up in the Conservative faith, went to an Orthodox-run Jewish day school, and married a Reform Jew. Like many Jews, I can do difference. We may not agree on everything, but we can find commonalities.

Judaism is inherently dialogic, a quality that's worth emulating. Discussion is crucial. Don't urge your kids to follow dogma or authority blindly. Don't tell them not to rock the boat. Don't urge them to stay in a narrow place. *Noodge* them to be fierce, both intellectually and in the pursuit of social justice. Urge them to follow in the footsteps of our forefather Jacob, the guy who wrestled with an angel. We don't all have to agree, but we have to respect each other's perspectives.

"Magnificent fractiousness," remember?

## IGNORE ANYONE WHO SAYS THERE'S ONLY ONE WAY TO RAISE A GREAT KID

Here you are, reading a chapter telling you to raise kids who seek out diverse opinions and don't give all that many hoots about the dominant paradigm. Therefore, I must add that you should feel free to ignore me, this book's authority figure.

As Ann Hulbert's superb book on the social history of parenting literature, *Raising America: Experts, Parents, and a Century of Advice About Children,* points out, there have *always* been twin threads of expert parenting advice in parenting literature: one more permissive and the other more authoritarian. These approaches are forever contradictory, and there are credentialed fancy-degreed experts in each theoretical camp and mothers who fervently believe that there is a single, holy, right way. There isn't. (Two Jews, three synagogues.) Right now, the terms "helicopter" and "free-range" express that dichotomy. People tend to twist the terms to fit whatever behaviors they want to criticize: Free-range parents are neglectful and never discipline their kids. Helicopter parents never give their kids the skills to be independent.

Forget these labels. You do you. But I hope you will use your own logic to consider the real risks and benefits of letting your kid stretch their tether, and figure out when it makes sense to offer more structure. (When my kids were younger, I used to roll my eyes at parents who begged and pleaded for their toddlers' cooperation and buy-in. My go-to expression was "They love the crate!" Older kids need practice in making choices and evaluating risk, but little kids are like dogs—they feel more secure when they know exactly where your limits are and what the rules are. We think of putting a dog in a crate as a punishment, but the dog quickly finds it soothing and familiar. And no, I am not literally suggesting you put your child in a crate, what is *wrong* with you?)

For real: Don't worry what I think; take all of social media with a grain of salt; and don't read articles about the latest study proving you are an ambulatory piece of poop as a parent. As ever, Dr. Benjamin Spock was right: Trust your instincts. You know more than you think you do. Ignore the clamor of contradictory authority figures and listen for your own inner voice.

Many moms today think that they are more criticized in their parenting than any generation has been before, but I don't think that's really true. Maybe social media has made mothers feel more judged, but I think know-it-alls and "concern trolls" (people who pretend to be moved by caring for your welfare, but actually want to make you feel bad about yourself and make themselves feel superior) have always existed, and they may have been even more likely to say things aggressively rather than passive-aggressively a few generations ago. My mom used to tell me about the earful she got—from all kinds of quarters—for waiting until the antediluvian age of twenty-six to have me. My dad's grandmother used to tell my mother she'd *deprived her* of ever meeting her great-grandchildren by waiting so long. (This turned out not to be the case—my great-grandmother lived to be 100 and died when I was in college—so eventually my great-grandmother switched gears and berated my mom for *depriving her* of the opportunity to dance at my wedding.) If it's not one thing, it's your mother.

## *60* Mamaleh Methodology

1. **Let your kid question you and question teachers—respectfully.** There's no excuse to be rude. And questioning is not the same thing as hectoring; no one likes a querulous, whining pain who isn't really interested in intellectual engagement, but rather just wants to express that liiiiiiiiife is unfaaaaaaaair. That's not a question.

2. **Cultural identity isn't a monolith; teach your kid that it comes in many flavors.** I'm personally only beginning to explore the vastness of Jewish tradition. My coworkers at *Tablet,* the Jewish magazine I work for, were gobsmacked that I'd never had shakshuka, a Sephardic (Middle Eastern) dish of eggs poached in tomato sauce. There's a "Shuka Truck" near our office, and we had to have a field trip for me to explore this staple of Israeli-Arab cuisine. (It was awesome, btw.) I still have so much to learn about Jewish music, history, and art. Whatever your background, you can always learn more. That's modeling intellectual curiosity to your kids, as well as the acknowledgment that the world is a diverse place and you (the central authority in your child's life) don't know everything.

3. **Do not read too many parenting books.** I mean, you can read this one. This one's cool. But in general, be a skeptic. Anyone who tells you there's only one right way to do anything—from raising children to reading for pleasure to chopping an onion—is not to be trusted. When someone hectors you—in person or in print—about child-rearing, try to retain or recapture your adolescent sense of "You're not the boss of me!"

4. Ponder the balancing act of group identity and diversity. It's important to teach children about their own heritage of accomplishment, empathy, good works, good humor, and *menschlichkeit* (the qualities of being a *mensch,* a good person). But it's also important to provide examples of ethical behavior, heroism, independent thinking, and standing up against unjust authority from other cultures. Liberally use literature and moral lessons from many sources ... and be an exemplar of the behavior you want to see in your child.

## Chapter 5

# Encourage Geekiness

The woods would be very silent if no birds sang except the best.

—*Yiddish proverb*

When I was in the baby/toddler parenting trenches, I often felt like Prometheus chained to the rock. I would look upward, grasping for sublime conversation, unable to muster anything but musings about the best brand of diaper-disposal canister. I would stoop, not to try to drink cool delicious water, but to pick up wads of cat hair from dusty corners.

Then, right when I most needed it, I met an enchanting nine-year-old boy, the child of friends. He was SO CUTE, so sweet and solicitous of the three younger kids who were at brunch when we met. He played soccer and he'd read all the Harry Potter books in one summer and he was just a delightful vision of what boys could be like, of what my own future could be like when my annoying tiny children finally got bigger. The boy was fascinated by my job and asked a ton of questions about it, because he wanted to be a journalist. He praised the fish my husband had caught on Lake Michigan, and ate his own metric weight in it, so we loved him more.

At the table, over bagels, he asked me, very seriously, "What do you think is more important, knowledge or imagination?" I looked at him, flabbergasted. "That's a great question," I hedged. He laughed, "Oh, I don't want you to think it was all *my* question. I was reading about Albert Einstein, and he said imagination was more important than knowledge, and I'm not sure he was right, so that's why I asked."

Holy crap.

This kid was, by most accountings, a geek. I imagine a lot of boys his own age gave him the side-eye. But so the hell what? He was lovely and brilliant and curious and polite, and I wanted to have him stuffed and mounted on my mantel. (Wait, that came out wrong.) It's unfortunate that we live in a world in which being philosophical or passionate about quirky things opens you up to mockery. We should encourage kids who want to ponder existential questions, who are interested in random things like the history of Day-Glo paint or the literary output of Isaac Bashevis Singer or what to feed cows to get the tastiest cheese. And we should help them understand that it takes a while to become an expert, it's fine to explore interests you're intrigued by but not skilled at yet, and learning curves are normal. You have to do the time and the work to become truly great at something. If you love to sing, sing (we don't expect the woods to be silent!), and if you remain serious about singing, you can study music and train your voice and become a better singer. If you are fascinated by the *Millennium Falcon,* study diagrams of it, build it out of LEGO, find fellow nerds who discuss its layout and engine functions. People with less imagination and more desire to follow the crowd may mock you for your passions, but screw them.

Passion and geekery were what drew me to my husband. He was working at the magazine *Wired* when it was just getting started; I was working at a magazine called *Sassy.* It was the early '90s, and Jonathan's job was to explain the Internet to people. His title was "Online Tsar." He asked if we could have coffee, so he could talk to me about interesting things my magazine could do on this newfangled thing called the World Wide Web. I was the only person at *Sassy* with an e-mail address, which I possessed only because I'd reported a story entitled "Is Cyberspace Safe for Girls?" (We said "cyberspace" with a straight face back then.) Jonathan flew from San Francisco to New York, and as we sat sipping cappuccinos, he talked about this visual communications medium I'd never even heard of, and I was enchanted by his fervor. He was a raver then, with long curly black hair and dangling earrings, and he wore purple and green like a jester. I was dressed all in black, standard New York City girl-editor drag. He matched no definition of cool that I knew, but his ardor for unfamiliar technology and music and media was incredibly attractive to me. The next day he came to my office to show me this World Wide Web doohickey. We needed my dial-up modem. He couldn't connect. When he left, my colleague Diane ran around the office singing, "Margie met her husband! Margie met her husband!" She was right.

## WHAT IS A GEEK, AND WHY DO YOU
## WANT ONE IN YOUR HOUSE?

The word *geek* comes from the German word *geck*, "fool." In the eighteenth and nineteenth centuries, a geek was a circus freak who bit the heads off chickens. The word *nerd*, on the other hand, is a modern one, invented by Dr. Seuss for his 1950 book *If I Ran the Zoo*. (It's one of the imaginary creatures, along with a Nerkle and a Seersucker, that the hero wanted to collect.)

Today, the notion of geekiness is being reclaimed and rehabbed. (The word itself isn't quite as far along in its reformation as *queer*, which went from a slur about gay people to a term of proud identification . . . but it's getting there.) To quote Jim MacQuarrie—a cartoonist, designer, writer, archery coach, and contributor to the blog Geek-Dad, "Being a geek is all about your own personal level of enthusiasm, not how your level of enthusiasm measures up to others. If you like something so much that a casual mention of it makes your whole being light up like a halogen lamp, if hearing a stranger fondly mention your favorite book or game is instant grounds for friendship, if you have ever found yourself bouncing out of your chair because something you learned blew your mind so hard that you physically could not contain yourself—you are a geek."

Being a geek means finding and exploring your passions, and allowing yourself to be obsessive, even if others find your obsessions uncool. Guess what? Cool is a lie. Obsessing about being cool means that you're always chasing something, forever uncertain, perpetually living in a state of Fear of Missing Out. Jews have historically been super-uncool. We are *schmucks, nebbishes, nudniks, schmoes, schmendriks, schlemiels, schlemazls.* (These Yiddish words all mean "dork" . . . though as with "nerd" and "geek," precise nuances vary.) Yet our dorkiness has served us well. Jewish mothers throughout time have encouraged their kids' interests and not cared who knew it. Popularity and conformity have not been our bag. Intellectual inspiration? That's where it is at.

We want our kids to put in the industry and effort of exploring their interests. Let kids know you care about them being inquisitive and thoughtful, seeking challenges and doing work for its own sake rather than to prove their smarty-pantsedness. This means we don't do our kids' homework for them or write their college essays; if, as a result, the kid doesn't do as well on his homework, so be it. (Ralph Waldo Emerson, not a Jew but still a lovely man, said, "Character is higher than intellect.")

I'm going to make the perhaps-shocking suggestion that you help your kid find their passion and worry more about nurturing that than you do about homework or test scores. The discipline we spoke of earlier in the book—applied to the work a child really cares about—is what I believe leads to the self-esteem we're going to talk about later in this chapter.

I suspect that Jews have long had a reputation for being brilliant when what we've really been was hardworking. I was amused by the notion in *Jewish Jocks,* a book coedited by my former *Tablet* colleague Marc Tracy, that even in the years when plenty of Jews were pro athletes (yes, they existed), Jews were always considered the brainiacs of the team. Were they actually smarter? Who knows? What they did was practice a ton and play with strategy. The Jews of pro basketball hustled, passed accurately, made outside shots precisely. They tended to be short compared to the other players, so it didn't make sense for them to try to get in there and mix it up with elbows and shoulders. The Jews of football were masters of if-then thinking. Brooklyn-bred Sid Luckman, a star quarterback for the Chicago Bears in the 1940s, turned down numerous athletic scholarships to attend Columbia University, where he paid full freight, before being drafted by the Bears. Known as "the first great T-formation quarterback," he spent hours at night memorizing thousands of different plays and scenarios. His employment of the T-formation changed the game. Today he still owns several Bears team records.

For Jewish mothers, the answer is to encourage the traits our grandparents' and great-grandparents' generations praised: morality, hard work, honesty, devotion to community. To put that in practical parenting terms, instead of praising our kids to the skies, we should work on helping them feel good about themselves by doing their best and helping them help others. We should make them feel smart not by telling them "You're so smart!" but by helping them identify and develop their specific interests.

As I've said before, we're entirely too worried about having our kids be happy. Stop saying and even thinking "the most important thing is that they're happy right now." (We're Jews. Happy is not our default state.) Too much worry about making your kid happy each moment leads to too little work on helping your kid develop the skills to be fulfilled for the rest of their life.

## HELP YOUR KID DISCOVER THEIR PASSIONS

Let your kids see your own geekery. My kids know that their daddy adores statistics, enjoys pondering correlation and causation and flawed studies, and loves asking about how things work: brewing ale, doing biochemical research, designing a 3-D printer. They know that I'm fascinated by the Triangle Shirtwaist Company factory fire and the origins of the labor movement, and that I love my job as a journalist because I get to immerse myself in other people's lives and stories.

Give your kid time to figure what it is they're really ardent about. Try different sports, crafts, kinds of books, activities. Pay attention to your kid's spark—what seems likely to light it up? Don't worry if your kid seems a little dreamy and unfocused or otherworldly. "All journeys have secret destinations of which the traveler is unaware," wrote the philosopher Martin Buber. Also, a 2012 study by scientists at the University of Wisconsin-Madison and at the Max Planck Institute for Human Cognitive and Brain Sciences found a direct correlation between the amount of day-dreaming a person does and that person's working memory capacity. The higher your working memory, the higher your reading comprehension and other measures of intelligence.

If your kid shows an affinity for something and you can afford extra classes in it, or teams or coaches, go for it. If you can't afford it (or if you're like me, and Hebrew school eats up two days a week), show your child you take their interests seriously, especially if they aren't *your* interests. (I keep thinking of the story told by John Boyega about telling his dad he'd gotten cast in the *Star Wars* reboot, and his dad shrieking and celebrating with him—"That is fantastic! I knew it!"—before asking, "What is *Star Wars*"?) A good dad applauds his kid's acting even if he has no clue about the world of acting. And the converse of Boyegan parenting is the horde of grown-ups who insist their children take violin because the parent regrets giving up on music lessons when they were ten.

Anyway. Urge your kid to pursue their passions, even if other people think those passions are uncool. Urge them to fight for social justice and stand up to bullying, even if their friends might think they're a goob. One reason Jewish children have become successful in science, the arts, and social justice fields is that we've been taught not to be afraid to be passionate, focused dweebs.

## YOU DON'T HAVE TO BE POPULAR, AND YOU DON'T HAVE TO DO POPULAR THINGS

There's a term in Jewish education called the Santa Pause. It's the time every December when Jewish kids realize they aren't like most of their friends, that they aren't part of the majority culture. It can be a bummer. But it can also be a great model for how to view our place in the world. It's okay to be Other! In all things, not just in Jewiness. It's okay to be a geek; it's okay to stand alone. When I was nine, the only girl on my Little League team, my mom explained the Equal Rights Amendment to me and sewed a women's lib patch (with a fist on it!) on my cap. This irked some of the Little League dads. But my mom explained to me how women had been denied the vote and the right to own property for a long time, and now there was a legal battle under way to bring fairness to our country, and me doing my best as a ballplayer in an entire field of boys could be part of that effort.

Finding an identity tied to the thing that makes you different and special can even help a kid find a place in the world. In *Little Failure,* the novelist Gary Shteyngart shares the true story of how as a youthful, not-very-acculturated, superdorky Russian immigrant, his newfound skill in writing terrible yet addictive science fiction made him marginally less loathed in school. "Don't get me wrong," he writes. "I'm still a hated freak. But here's what I'm doing: I am redefining the terms under which I am a hated freak. I am moving the children away from my *Russianness* and toward storytelling. . . . 'Did you write anything new?' shouts a kid in the morning, a merchant's son, renowned for his lack of basic literacy. 'Will the Lopezians attack? What's Dr. Omar gonna do next?' "

Encourage your kid to feel good when she's truly done something worthwhile or difficult, like working hard on a sci-fi story, stopping her friends from publicly bullying another kid (even if that puts your kid in the line of fire), being brave in a scary situation.

When Maxie was three, another kid broke her nose while she was at preschool. (Accidentally. Probably. Allegedly.) Both kids had been riding in plastic toy cars in the school playground, and he rammed into her so hard she slammed her face into her dashboard, then slipped under the car, and he ran over her. That's life in the big city. Maxie had to go to the ENT several times after that, which wasn't fun. The third time, she was quivery but didn't cry in the cab, and then the appointment went fine. She got a toy from the giveaway box, so she was in a pretty perky mood on the way home. I said, "You know, you were pretty brave. You were scared, but you held it together, and I'm proud of you." She replied in the manner of a child who watches a lot of television (again, just want to reassure you that I am a deeply flawed parent here) and who never forgets a single idiom, "That was not nearly as bad as I anticipated! Now, who's up for canasta? Or should I say FUNasta?" (I Googled when I got home. The canasta thing was a line from *The Fairly OddParents*.)

## THE VERY WORD *SELF-ESTEEM* MAKES ME WANT TO HURL

Abraham Joshua Heschel (1907–1972), the great rabbi and civil rights leader who marched with Dr. Martin Luther King Jr., said, "When you are young, start working on this great work of art called your own existence. One . . . remember the importance of self-discipline; second, study the great sources of wisdom . . . and, third, remember that life is a celebration, or can be a celebration."

Discipline, study, celebration. Note that Heschel did not add "Feel awesome about yourself!" We need to stop worrying so much about kids' self-esteem and start worrying more about how our kids will create meaning in their lives.

Help your child in their quest for meaning. Don't try to bolster their sense of self by applauding stuff that's essentially meaningless. If they are over the age of two, do not coo at them, "I like the way you used your words!" If they got a good score on a dumb multiple-choice test you know they didn't study for, don't celebrate it. Tell your children what is expected of them, and after you have told them what is expected of them, stop cheerleading when they do what they're supposed to do. To continue to praise *congratulations-you're-not-an-asshole* behavior is like cooing and proffering a catnip mouse every time your cat uses the litter box.

You know what else you shouldn't praise besides braininess and not acting like a dick? Generosity! A series of studies by psychology professor Joan Grusec and others at the University of Toronto found that kids who are often praised for generosity actually wind up being *less* generous than other kids. To them, generosity becomes something you do to earn praise, not a thing you *are.*

An aside: I originally wanted to call this chapter "Screw the Self-Esteem Movement." Historically, Jewish mothers have not told their children they're brilliant and kind and gorgeous and spectacular. To a degree, that was so we wouldn't tempt the evil eye, *ptui ptui ptui.* It is fine, though, for us to blush and beam while our children's *grandparents* talk about how brilliant and kind and gorgeous and spectacular our children are. Boasting is the prerogative of *bubbes* and *zaydes.*

Stanford psychologist Carol Dweck (who you'll read more about in the next chapter) did groundbreaking research in why we shouldn't praise our kids for being smart. In a typical experiment, she'd ask a kid to solve a puzzle. Sometimes she'd tell the child they were brilliant; sometimes she didn't. The kids who weren't told they were smart were excited to tackle harder and harder puzzles, and more confident in their abilities to solve them . . . which actually made them better puzzle solvers. The kids who were told they were smart usually wanted to quit while they were ahead; they became afraid that if they tackled harder puzzles they'd fail, and thereby prove themselves not-smart. The moral: Do not tell your kid they're smart; tell them you're proud when they keep trying.

It's not as if intelligence is the most important indicator of success in life, anyway. Psychologist Louis Terman, the guy who came up with the Stanford-Binet test and invented the term "IQ," was famous for his longitudinal study of smart kids. Starting in 1921, he began following over a thousand kids whose IQs tested at 135 or higher. Terman died in 1959, but the study participants (affectionately known as "Termites") are still being followed today; the study will end when the last Termite dies. Terman clearly wanted to believe that high IQ was highly correlated with success, but the data didn't cooperate. He and his colleagues and successors found that persistence, confidence, and encouragement were the most important factors in adult achievement. Encouragement, incidentally, isn't synonymous with praise. It means urging kids to keep trying and giving them opportunities to learn and succeed. The big takeaway here: Intelligence is not the difference that makes a difference.

Years ago I interviewed a psychology professor named Brian Goldman at Clayton State University, another self-esteem researcher. In our chat, he made the distinction between "fragile high self-esteem" and "secure high self-esteem." People with fragile high self-esteem love themselves, but their love stands on shaky ground: It's entirely dependent on what others think of them. They have a hard time acknowledging their weaknesses, so they're unable to work on meaningful self-improvement. You can't develop a secure sense of who you are if you don't acknowledge your limitations, and you can't do *that* if you feel your essential self-worth is being challenged whenever you're criticized or think you failed at something. People with secure high self-esteem, on the other hand, acknowledge their strengths *and* their weaknesses. They're less likely to be swayed by external forces because they know who they really are. Ladies and gentlemen, I give you geeks.

## URGE SATISFACTION FOR A JOB WELL DONE

I used to offer reflexive, drag-queen-like bursts of "fabulous!" every time Josie showed me a finger painting. But I realized before long that neither of us was paying much attention—she had come to expect the praise, and I was on autopilot. So I dialed it back. I started following the advice of Alfie Kohn, an educational theorist I often disagree with . . . but I liked his ideas about what to say instead of rhapsodizing by rote. In *Punished by Rewards: The Trouble with Gold Stars, Incentive Plans, A's, Praise, and Other Bribes,* Kohn warns about kids becoming "praise junkies," perpetually needing their next fix of compliments and becoming dependent on other people to evaluate what they've done. He suggests that instead of praising kids' work, adults describe it without judging. Upon looking at my child's painting, I could, for instance, say, "Wow, you made the vampire bunny's fangs really big!" or "How'd you make this puddle of innards look so goopy?" Instead of praising Maxie for getting dressed without help in the morning, I could just observe, "You got dressed by yourself! In stripes *and* polka dots!" (Someone invented a little button that said "I got dressed by myself today!," which is a work of don't-blame-me parenting genius.)

Kohn also suggests that parents and teachers ask questions to help kids reflect on what they've done rather than applauding it. You could say, "Which part of the sculpture was the hardest to make?" or "Why'd you choose the colors you did?" or "Who'd you work with? Which parts did each of you do? How was collaborating?" And when a kid does something kind or caring for another person, point out how the behavior affects the other person: "Did you see Shirley's face? She was so happy when you helped her build that sand castle."

As your kids get older, you can get tougher. I have clashed with teenage Josie over the fact that she'll ask me to read a homework assignment the night before it's due, and I'll hand it back if I find a couple of punctuation errors or dangling modifiers. "Proof it before you give it to me," I say, and she sometimes rolls her eyes and snatches the paper back and complains about my being too critical. But I think Josie knows that when I praise her work (unlike Kohn, I am not entirely antipraise; I'm just *selective* with praise), I really mean it.

Constructive feedback may not be what you're looking for when you just want someone to say your work is amazing and marvelous and don't change a damn thing. But come on, you and I both know most work is rarely great. When your kid gets out into the real world, they're going to get real criticism and comments. They'd better be able to deal without crumpling like a wet Kleenex. It may not always feel like it, but honest appraisal is your friend. And your kid's. These days when I get enthused about one of Maxie's paintings or one of Josie's debate speeches, they know I'm not faking. The praise means more.

Reserve your most enthusiastic praise for when your kid does something good without expecting a reward. Maybe one sibling put away the other sibling's laundry. Or maybe your daughter helped a classmate with homework on the phone or was patient with an annoying toddler visitor or made strenuous efforts to make sure everyone felt included on a sleepover. Or your son read to his little cousin or went through his clothing drawers to take out the outgrown items without being asked. These are things worth being impressed by—not a grade on a test.

You can also praise the behavior you admire in others. If there's an example of righteous or brave behavior in the news or in a book you're reading, talk about it. In our neighborhood a couple of years ago, there was a giant explosion caused by an illegal gas hookup. It killed two people. It was a sad and scary time. But we watched the video of the explosion, and we saw the people running toward, not away from, the big cloud of smoke. We watched an off-duty fireman—an older guy with a belly—scamper up a fire escape and start banging on windows to make sure no one was trapped inside. We talked about the little siblings of one of Josie's classmates who lived a half block away, who had been across the street when the disaster happened; a stranger herded them into a deli and fed them and kept them safe and entertained until they could be reunited with their family. This is the kind of behavior we want our kids to emulate. Worry about building a kid who is good, not a kid who has good self-esteem.

Revel in your kid's virtuousness, hard work, and mastery of difficult emotions. It's normal for kids to have big feelings of sadness, rage, jealousy, shame. What's impressive is being able to talk about the feelings (instead of lashing out), figure out self-soothing strategies, or manage to leave the room or do deep breathing exercises when all you want is to Hulk out. When Maxie was six and the school year was winding to a close, she worked herself into a lather at bedtime, sobbing about swimming lessons at the camp she was to attend. She couldn't even tell me why she was stressed, but it was clear she was worried about being pushed past what she felt capable of. But then she figured out how she could regain her self-possession. She got out of bed and brought me a book of temporary tattoos. She said, "A tattoo will help me calm down. The warm water on my arm will distract me and then I can look at the pretty tattoo and feel happy." So I gave her a tattoo of a violet, and rubbed her arm gently, for somewhat longer than was perhaps strictly necessary for fake-tattoo adhesion. She chilled out enough to let me ask her what, exactly, was frightening her. When she told me she was afraid of being forced to dive, I countered with the story of my own camp experience at the YMCA in Rhode Island, where a counselor tricked me into tucking my chin into my chest and pushed me into the pool after telling me he wouldn't. (Dick.) I promised I'd e-mail the camp director about making sure no one did that to her. She told me she was worried about treading water, and I reminded her that she'd just done so for a long time at the JCC pool. I commended her for figuring out how to gather her composure and talk to me about her worries. She was anxious about who her swim teacher would be, and I couldn't tell her, since she wouldn't be assigned a group until she arrived at camp, but I could say, "We'll cross that bridge when we come to it." True to form, Maxie was soon repeating "We'll cross that bridge when we come to it!" about everything.

Self-esteem can also come from self-control, from making the choice to delay gratification or an explosion, from knowing you're doing something that's difficult. My dad was a psychiatrist who worked with the profoundly mentally ill. I joke that I am the only child of a psychiatrist who is sane. I think I'm (relatively?) emotionally healthy—precisely because my father wasn't interested in garden-variety neurosis. I didn't grow up under a therapeutic, micromanaged, superjudgy microscope, because my fairly normal *mishegas* (craziness) wasn't really on his radar. My dad worked with homeless schizophrenics, troubled youth in group homes, and dementia patients in nursing homes. He didn't care if people smelled horrible; he didn't pull back when they were hallucinating and ranting. He *really* liked crazy people. There was only one psychiatristy thing he did regularly when I was a kid. When my brother and I were starting to poke and snarl at each other, or when we were starting to get worked up and agitated, he taught us to stop, find him, and announce "I want some attention." I recall being told to say this when I was five and my brother was three. I think it started earlier. My dad conveyed to us that we could control our behavior, that we had the skills to recognize when we were starting to lose control before we got unhinged, and that he was there to help us if we needed distraction.

## DOGS SENSE FEAR, AND KIDS SENSE HYPOCRISY

Even those of us who know that self-esteem isn't a worthy goal in and of itself want to instill ethical values in our kids . . . but then we often fail to walk the walk. There's a rhetoric/reality gap at play. We tell kids we cherish effort, honesty, kindness. But our testimony isn't played out in what we *show* our kids we value.

The Making Caring Common Project is an annual

survey of over ten thousand middle and high school students conducted by the Harvard Graduate School of Education. The schools are a mix of urban, suburban, and rural and public and private. The kids come from a mix of socioeconomic and ethnic backgrounds. The 2014 study asked students how they viewed their parents' child-raising priorities in terms of happiness, achievement, and caring for others:

- A whopping 54 percent reported that achievement was their parents' top priority.
- Nearly two-thirds said that parents and peers alike would rank achievement above caring for others.
- Students were three times more likely to agree than disagree with the statement: "My parents are prouder if I get good grades in my classes than if I'm a caring community member in class and school."

If your kid is correct in her belief that you care more about her accomplishments than her thoughtfulness, you've got a parenting problem. Is the world truly such a vicious place that if your kid doesn't grab the biggest slice of the pie, she will be entirely without pie? Is there only one path to success and fulfillment in life? If I waved data at you about wealth not ensuring happiness (research indicates that we all have a happiness "set point," and changes in the environment don't seem to affect all that much—unless we become truly poor or truly sick), or yapped at you about grades and test scores not being a great predictor of success or joy, would you believe me? Ponder these questions and get back to me.

I don't want to live in a world in which selfishness is the

rule. I tell my kids to do the right thing even if another kid is doing the wrong one. I like that my kids have always gone to schools where teachers and administrators talk about obligations to others, commitments to community and teams, learning to work together. As the Making Caring Common folk ask, "Do we place consistent ethical demands on our children not only when it collides with their happiness and achievements but when they may be furious at us, when it threatens our own happiness?"

When we sweep in to solve our kids' problems and try to cushion them from every bump on the way to adulthood, we keep them from learning the coping strategies that ultimately make them competent, self-sufficient, and kind. Teaching your kid to look out for number one means you're actually harming his ability to make and sustain strong relationships and a strong sense of self. That's where healthy self-esteem comes from. Being a geek—finding culture or activities you love, immersing yourself in them, working to better your skills and knowledge, finding a community of like-minded people—is more important than ephemeral grades or the evasion of consequences.

## IS THE BODY THE SELF?

A final point: It's hard for kids to develop a healthy sense of self if their mothers don't have one. We women tend to drop-kick ourselves when we've screwed up. Many of us criticize our faces, hair, wrinkles, moods, and any less than perfect part of our bodies in a way we'd never do to our kids'. I worry that today thinness has taken the moral place in our lives that good works used to have. When I was in my early twenties (and skinny!), I read Joan Jacobs Brumberg's *The Body Project* and had my tiny mind blown. The book looks at girls' diaries from 1830 on and compares what girls saw as important over time. Where once girls wrote about respectfulness, kindness, warm-heartedness, and piety, by the 1980s they associated "goodness" almost exclusively with their own bodies, exercise, and eating habits. They often cared far more about appearance than about other people. This is problematic. I think it's important for families to go on walks and bike rides together, and to make healthy food choices whenever possible, but to focus over-much on the body as opposed to the soul won't make anyone happier or healthier. Assigning moral value to food is both weird and a privilege of a particularly privileged class.

I'm reminded of an *Inside Amy Schumer* skit in which young women in a restaurant talk about what they've eaten and moan, "I'm so bad!" It becomes pretty quickly clear that their values are a teensy bit skewed. One character starts, "I was cyberbullying my niece on Instagram the other day and I literally ate fifteen minimuffins! I'm so bad!" Another responds, "Yesterday after I knelt on my gerbil to hear what sound it would make, I, like, wasn't thinking and ate a ball of mozzarella like it was a peach! I am so bad!" Etc. The young women all reassure each other that they're *not* bad because they have a thigh gap. Then they eat the waiter.

There's a value in Judaism called *shmirat haguf*—taking care of the body. It's important. Our bodies are a gift, created in God's image. We should treat our corporeal selves kindly. "It is man's duty to avoid whatever is injurious to the body and cultivate habits conducive to health and vigor," wrote the twelfth-century sage Maimonides, who was also a physician. (He wrote quite a bit about the benefits of chicken soup, the ultimate Jewish health food.) Respect your body by feeding it well, moving it around, treating sex with the respect it deserves.

Mothers can help their daughters become confident women by refraining from body commentary (it bugs me even when someone talks about my daughter's "cute little figure"—even if it's intended to be complimentary, it's objectifying), and pointing out that women's bodies throughout history have been subject to creepy scrutiny. We can help our sons become confident men by teaching them to respect women and not be shallow doofuses. Teach all kids to apologize when they do something wrong, but not to do so obsessively. (Guess which gender is more likely to apologize obsessively.)

I realize I'm telling you to conduct a balancing act—make sure your kid feels supported and loved without overpraising them or rescuing them every time they're in trouble. Encourage them to be a geek, but be sure they also live in their body. In urging you to raise a geek kid you may feel left out—as you may wind up encouraging the kid to pursue interests you don't share.

Courage, dear heart. Parents have always struggled, both with balance and with the worry that we're screwing up. The Hasidic teacher Simha Bunim (1765–1827) once said, "Everyone must have two pockets, so that he can reach into the one or the other according to his needs. In the right pocket should be the words: *'For my sake the world was created,'* and in the left, *'I am dust and ashes.'*" Whenever we feel depressed and without value, we should look at the first note. When we start to believe that we're utterly awesome, we should look at the second.

## 𝒪𝒪 Mamaleh Methodology

1. **Don't mock nerdiness.** Praise it. Point out when "making fun of the nerd" is used as lazy shorthand in pop culture—this happens a lot in live-action TV aimed at kids. (It's actually less common in good cartoons. A single song in the delightful *Phineas & Ferb*—in reruns on Disney as I type this—uses the words *infernal, invective, abhor, ambivalence, subjective, atrocious,* and *apathy.* Cartoons need not rot your children's brains—especially if they're cartoons with nerd heroes.)

2. **Point out examples of creativity and problem solving.** Show kids those contests in which kids make prom dresses out of duct tape. Check out blogs in which people modify IKEA furniture in quirky ways. Share stories about people who got out of difficult spots by using logic, strategy, or innovative thinking.

3. **Give your kid toys that nurture imaginative, open-ended, creative play.** LEGO. Playmobil. Train tracks. Blocks. Craft kits. Crayons and paints. Games that require strategy rather than racking up a high body count. By the time your kid is a tween or teen, you won't have much control over the media they consume outside your house, so set the groundwork early. You can refuse to buy toys that aren't congruent with your values, but if a teen or tween wants to use their own money to buy a game that makes you roll your eyes, make sure this is a hill you want to die on. And remember that if a kid watches dumb TV or plays a violent first-person shooter at someone else's house, it's not the end of the world.

4. **Initiate conversations about justice and fairness, so your kids know what your values are.** We assume our kids know what we care about, simply because they steep in the values of their surroundings. We are not always correct. Be explicit about what matters to you.

5. **Embrace your own inner nerd.** Let your kid see you doing crafts, experimenting for fun with recipes, dancing in the living room to music they find utterly horrifying, taking classes for your own edification.

6. **Walk the walk.** Don't bemoan your own stupidity (I'm totally guilty of this when it comes to math); don't wail about your own thighs; don't obsess about your screwups in the presence of your kids. And don't yell at your significant other for their screwups; be a helper who works at fixing what's gone awry.

## Chapter 6

# Emphasize—
# but Don't Fetishize—
# Education

Don't look for more honor than your learning merits.

—*Yiddish proverb*

When Josie was almost six, she desperately tried to teach Maxie, then almost three, to read. Despite Josie's pedagogical efforts, Max was not interested. The more I protested— "Josie, she's too little! She doesn't get it! You couldn't read when you were two either! You can teach her when she's older!"—the more frustrated Josie got. Max, already aware of how to push her sister's buttons, began refusing even to look at the books, demurely turning her eyes away as Josie begged, "Look! Please! Max, just look!" Finally, Josie lost it and screamed, "YOU ARE GOING TO BE THE DUMBEST BABY IN YOUR SCHOOL!"

Sadly, there are parents out there who behave like my five-year-old. They want their precious babies to be the best in their school, to have a leg up on the competition, to be perceived as gifted. They don't want real intellectual curiosity and quirk; they want a Best in Show medal.

I include Jews among those I'm condemning. Many of us have lost the outsider's perspective that has actually made us successful as a people. Come back to the fold and learn your history, my people! Learn from our past, people who are not my people! Education has always been an important part of Jewish accomplishment, but it's not the whole enchilada. The role of school is to supplement the values discussed throughout this book: independence, self-discipline, intellectual curiosity, storytelling, laughter, social action, and spirituality.

If you are in the fortunate position of having choices about where your child goes to school, try not to get caught up in modern-day bad-pedagogy madness. Schools that determine "giftedness" by test scores (not to mention tying teachers' and principals' compensation to test scores) help create a world in which deep, wide-ranging, multidisciplinary, multifaceted learning is sacrificed in favor of teaching kids how to fill in little bubbles. What you wind up with is kids who aren't engaged in learning. This is not the Jewish way.

Good grades and good test scores are not the end game. There's a reason child prodigies don't often become adult stars; at some point, it's not enough to perform on cue and deliver obediently whatever your teacher asks for. You have to stop parroting other artists, writers, musicians, scientists. You have to create new paradigms, new styles . . . which means making mistakes, irking the establishment, being misunderstood. Your teacher may actually find you kind of unnerving and annoying. You can't expect praise or compliments. You have to have a core sense of self to keep going, a desire to explore and let your own ideas achieve peak brilliance. *This* is the Jewish way.

There is no one perfect school. Some kids go to traditional, nonprogressive schools and learn good values and do great. Other kids go to kumbaya schools and are lazy entitled dickheads who vape so much they forget where the cafeteria is. There are excellent reasons to choose a Jewish day school and excellent reasons to choose a public school. There is no one-size-fits-all approach to education—there's only ways of learning that work for your kid, *and are supplemented by you,* ways that answer the "whys" and teach your kid to ask more "whys." There's a Yiddish proverb: "You can't control the wind, but you can adjust your sails." Your school choice may be limited by geography or money or access. Your kid may not be the kind of learner you expected. But then it's up to you to change tack.

## STOP FOCUSING ON THE WRONG METRICS OF SMARTNESS

Kids should not be asked to perform like beachball-balancing seals. When we focus on win-win-win achieve-achieve-achieve, we lose out on enjoying the process of learning and turning it into a lifelong habit.

We need to take a step back and look around at our schools. A huge problem with high-pressure, class-rank-obsessed, test-oriented schools is *cheating.* The Josephson School of Ethics does a comprehensive survey of American high school students every two years. Its 2012 survey of twenty-three thousand high school students found that 51 percent admitted cheating on a test in the last year, even as 99 percent of them said "It is important for me to be a person with good character." Ninety-three percent said they were satisfied with their own ethics and character; and 81 percent said that when it came to doing what is right, they believed they were better than most people they knew. *Hello, disconnect much?* Parents and schools are clearly doing something wrong when 32 percent of kids had deliberately plagiarized from the Internet for an assignment and 51 percent had copied someone else's homework. We need to let kids know that as long as they do their best work, it's okay not to ace every test.

Schools—public, private, and parochial—should offer multilevel instructional approaches, create a climate of tolerance that discourages bullying, and nurture appreciation of diversity and a wide variety of different kinds of smarts. The fact that Jews tend to do well on standardized tests gives us legitimacy in saying that standardized tests shouldn't have too much power. Tests shouldn't be used for purposes (promotion, punishment, etc.) for which they weren't designed—which is unfortunately what's happening now across the country. Tests that are supposed to give an overall picture of a school, to guide teacher development and training, or to help principals concretely support struggling classes are instead determining the fates of students and triggering huge sanctions against a school or financial rewards for individual teachers and principals whose students do well. All this can induce people to cheat—a *most* un-Jewish value.

Psychologist Carol Dweck (you remember her from the last chapter) has conducted study after study showing that kids who are praised for their brilliance and achievements wind up caring far more about their grades than about learning. Kids who think intelligence is a fixed trait (something you have or you don't) are more likely to shy away from challenges, with their attendant possibility of failure, than kids who think intelligence is malleable (something you can develop, like a muscle). Kids who think of intelligence as a muscle are less worried about looking dumb, more willing to take risks, better equipped to cope with failure. They're interested in the journey, not just the destination. When it comes to real-world success, research indicates that character and perseverance matter more than brilliance.

Remember the expression *al tifrosh min ha-tzibur,* from Chapter 2? Don't separate yourself from the community? We Jews have always made sure to have burial societies and children's aid charities; our prayers are written overwhelmingly in the first person plural, not the first person singular. But the kind of education that values standardized testing above all is the furthest thing from communitarian. Wealthy families buy tutoring. Upper-middle-class kids come into school with the huge advantage of being read to more often at home. Testing enforces existing divisions and even increases them. Being a Jewish mother means you shouldn't just worry about your kids; you should be concerned about *everyone's* kids. That means working to improve all schools—yes, even if your kid goes to a private or Jewish day school—in meaningful ways, because for us, education is inseparable from morality.

## SHUT UP ABOUT YOUR GIFTED CHILD

I hate to break this to you, but your kid is not gifted. At least, them's the odds. According to the National Association for

Gifted Children, only 6 to 10 percent of U.S. children are legitimately gifted. (Other experts think the number is even smaller.) Come on, most kids test into gifted programs when they're four. Guess what kinds of kids take these tests? Kids who have savvy, well-off parents. Some very smart little kids simply can't sit still for a two-hour test, or have separation anxiety or shyness around strange adults, or aren't privileged enough to have parents who know that the tests even exist. One study found that only 45 percent of the kids who scored 130 or higher on the Stanford-Binet would do so again if tested on another day. Not surprising. A friend of mine's very bright child tanked on the test for Hunter College Elementary School because the test was administered in a psychologist's home office and she had a cat in the next room. The kid couldn't focus on the questions because there was nearby meowing. He loved cats. All he could focus on was KITTY KITTY KITTY.

As it turns out, learning the alphabet early—even learning to read early—is not correlated with reading skill (or more important, reading enjoyment) later on. With apologies to Josie and her goals for baby Maxie, it's time to stop stressing doing stuff early (learning to read, moving from picture books to chapter books, being in the fancy class that whizzes through world history more speedily, taking as many advanced classes and national tests as early in your high school career as humanly possible). It's a wiser long-term course of action to teach a kid that books and learning are fun. Forget about labels. Focus on enjoying learning.

I'm over parents bragging about how their little geniuses read too well for picture books. I'm over parents rolling their eyes at graphic novels as "not really *books*" and bemoaning the influence of Captain Underpants and Wimpy Kid books as disrespectful of authority and generally trashy. (If they're Harold Bloom, they're even snotty about the literary wor- thiness of Harry Potter. Don't make me hurt you, Harold Bloom.) I'm over parents bragging about their children's stratospheric reading levels, demanding "harder" books, yanking "too easy" books from their children's hands. Argh.

## HOW TO SUPPORT YOUR KID'S SCHOOLING

For your kid to be a flexible thinker and a good human, you should choose a school that values *play,* if at all possible. "Play is the exultation of the possible," Martin Buber said. Many parents get anxious that their kid will be put at a disadvantage if he or she is not slaving over a hot textbook every night. But for elementary-school kids, the evidence that tons of homework is useful simply isn't there. Accord- ing to a 2001 review of more than 120 studies of homework and its effects by researchers at Duke University, there's lit- tle connection between amount of homework and achieve- ment in elementary school.

As kids get older, there's more support for the notion of homework—it helps kids develop responsibility and good study habits—but *only* if there's not too much. Harris Coo- per, the director of Duke's Program in Education, recom- mends that schools assign no more than ten minutes of homework per grade per night. In other words, ten minutes of homework for a first grader, twenty minutes for a second grader, up to a maximum of two hours for a twelfth grader. *More than that and not only do the benefits stop, the work may even prove deleterious.* Kids should have *lives.* And fun. And it's not just Cooper who feels this way; his recommendations are echoed by the National Education Association and the National PTA. If you have the luxury of choice, choose a school where incessant homework is not a *thing*. If you don't have that choice, consider working to educate your school community that hours of homework aren't beneficial for anyone.

Honestly, there have been a few times when I've simply opted out. Once, in first grade, Josie had an assignment to build a model of New York State's waterways out of crumpled paper towels on a baking sheet, then flood it to show the direction of water flow.

I'm sorry, my kid's in first grade! Who's supposed to do this assignment, exactly? Josie was hysterical with anxiety about it, but I refused to do it with (*for*) her. I don't know jack about New York State's waterways. I turn on the tap and water comes out. Why is there homework that requires Googling in first grade? I wrote a note to the teacher saying we weren't doing the assignment and explained to Josie (over her wails) that this was my line in the sand (or rather, my line in wet paper towels). I am happy to make and send hot chocolate for everyone on the skating trip; I will willingly volunteer in and raise money for the school library; I will buy extra school supplies to keep in the classroom for kids whose families can't afford them. But I will not mound sopping sheets of Bounty atop a baking sheet to depict the Catskill watershed.

So how do you help your kid do well, if not by screaming at them to finish their zillion hours of homework a night, doing their homework for them, and/or putting them in the most high-powered school you can find? Check out Amanda Ripley's *The Smartest Kids in the World and How They Got That Way*. This densely researched book crunches the actual data about parental involvement and schooling. Ripley looked at PISA (Programme for International Student Assessment) studies of schools and kids around the world to see which ones made kids the most accomplished and successful. Some commonalities: Parents who read to young children every day or almost every day wound up having kids who performed much better in reading by the time they were fifteen. These kids scored an average of *twenty-five points higher* on PISA's reading test (the average score is 500) than kids who weren't regularly read to—the equivalent of almost a full year of learning. More affluent parents were more likely to read to their children, but among families within the same socioeconomic group, the kids who were read to scored better than their peers.

As kids got older, the parental involvement that seemed to be most effective was pretty relaxed. Helicopter parenting—spending a lot of time in your kid's classroom—was not correlated with student achievement. You know what was? Talking to kids about movies, books, and current affairs. Teenagers with parents who had thoughtful discussions with them turned out to be better readers.

Talking about values and the wider world with your kid teaches the kid to become a thinking person. It tells him or her that you care enough to have meaningful conversations together, and it pushes him or her to be able to articulate opinions and defend them. These results were clear and convincing, even across different countries and different income levels: Fifteen-year-olds whose parents talked about complicated social issues with them not only scored better on the PISA but reported enjoying reading more overall.

Furthermore, parents who read for pleasure at home, on their own, were much likelier to have kids who liked to read and did it a lot. Again, this was true across income levels and in very different countries. Kids could see what parents valued, and it mattered more than anything parents *said*. And most parents aren't readers. Only four in ten parents in the PISA survey said they regularly read at home for enjoyment.

## A BRIEF HISTORY OF JEWISH EDUCATION

Historically, Jews have kicked butt academically. This is a fact. Much of modern Western education is based on old-school Jewish education, because why wouldn't you listen to the brainiac people? Back in 64 CE, Joshua ben Gamla, a high priest in Judea, decreed that every district and town was required to provide teachers for young children (as opposed to depending on the parents to teach them) and also ordered that children enter school at the age of six or seven. This eventually became standard operating procedure in much of the educated world. Starting in the eighteenth century, when the Enlightenment ushered in a more tolerant era, and Jews were allowed to attend government schools in Europe and create secular schools of their own, Jews started contributing to ideas about how best to educate children of all backgrounds. And America's National Education Association has cited the Talmud as its source for maximum class size topping out at twenty-five students.

Something that's always mattered to us Jews, something that doesn't seem to be part of modern education these days, sadly, is: Make early childhood education fun. I can't recall a time when I *didn't* know the once-upon-a-time story of what happened on a child's first day of school back in olden days. The teacher would put a drop of honey on the child's tongue, so that his first taste of learning would be sweet. That way, he begins as you wish him to continue.

I suspect everyone who ever went to a Jewish day school knows this story, but I didn't know its genesis until I started researching this book. I found that the story dates from *Sefer HaRokeach, The Book of Perfume,* written by Rabbi Eleazar of Worms (1160–1230). Fun fact: The book has nothing to do with perfume. (Or worms.) Eleazar and Rokeach have the same numerical value in the Hebrew-letter-to-number code system called *gematria;* calling the book *Sefer HaRokeach* was a mnemonic device to help people remember the author's name. (Fun fact number two: As a kid, I was obsessed with *gematria.* We passed notes in my Jewish day school written in *gematria* as secret code; I spent a lot of boring lesson time figuring out the numerical values of the names of dozens of celebrities I had crushes on and trying to make them align with the numerical value of my name, thus proving we were destined to be together. This, ladies and gentlemen, is why Jews are good with numbers.)

Anyway: *The Book of Perfume* is a little more expansive on the honey story. It says that customarily children were brought to learn for the first time on Shavuot, the holiday that commemorates the occasion upon which God gave the Hebrews the Torah at Mount Sinai. On that special first day of school, the rabbi brought a slate with the alef-bet, the Hebrew alphabet, written on it. The rabbi would put a little honey on the slate and the child would lick the honey off the letters. Then the child got a honey cake, upon which was inscribed, "The Lord God gave me a skilled tongue to know . . ." (Isaiah 50: 4–5). The rabbi would read the words, the child would repeat them, and then yum, cake.

Then the kid would get a hard-boiled egg, with these words written on it: "Human being, feed your stomach and fill your belly with this scroll, and I ate it and it tasted as sweet as honey to me" (Ezekiel 3:3). The rabbi would read the text, the child would repeat, and then hey, tasty egg.

Associating learning from a very young age with honey, cake, and a nifty egg with writing on it makes learning seem pretty enticing. We are a people who appreciate food.

## LEARNING SHOULD NOT BE A GRIND

The fourteenth-century *Menorat HaMaor,* published a couple of centuries after *Sefer HaRokeach,* echoes the notion that education should be associated with joy. "The parent must try to make the learning of Torah a pleasant experience for the child," its author Isaac Aboab exhorted. "He must see what the child likes and desires and use these things to reward the child for his studies. In this way the child will be conditioned to study willingly." Tiny children should not be using flash cards or going to "academic kindergarten" to be drilled on handwriting. Joy is what sets the scene for future engagement and interest in learning.

Of course, in earlier times, education was only for wee dudes. Judaism has long had a girl problem. For much of our history, girls and women were responsible for learning enough text and tradition to keep the *mitzvot,* the commandments, and teach them to her own very small children. A girl was supposed to grow into an *eishet chayil,* a woman of valor, who led by example and raised good children. Formal education was not, in the beginning, for them.

This changed in the early nineteenth century, when

Grace Aguilar became a big influence in education. A British Jewish novelist, she'd studied philosophy, French literature, music, ancient Greek history, and Josephus's history of the Jews of the Roman Empire. She embraced and expanded upon the notion that *mothers,* not rabbis, were a child's earliest teachers. Texts weren't necessarily the best way to educate children; mothers could teach in a far more engaging way through stories, moral lessons, and personal examples. She acknowledged that getting a kid to focus wasn't always easy. In "Hints on the Religious Instruction of the Hebrew Youth," from *The Spirit of Judaism* (1842), she wrote: "To instruct young children in the dull routine of daily lessons, to force the wandering mind to attention, the unwilling spirit to subjection, to bear with natural disinclination to irksome tasks, all this, as a modern writer very justly observes, is far more attractive in theory than in practice. It is a drudgery for which even some mothers themselves have not sufficient patience!" Damn, Grace. Truth.

In America, wealthy Jews tended to focus on secular education until 1838, when Rebecca Gratz took the Protestant Sunday school model and made a Jewish copy of it. She was a Philadelphian, a real go-getter, and a charitable dynamo. She started an organization to help the families of Revolutionary War vets when she was only twenty years old and launched a Hebrew Benevolent Society to aid poor women and children shortly after that. (She was also a stone cold fox and reputedly the model for Rebecca, the noble Jewish girl in *Ivanhoe.* The story goes that Washington Irving, a friend of the Gratz family, told his pal Sir Walter Scott about how fabulous Rebecca Gratz was, and Scott used her character in his book. Alas, Ivanhoe still winds up with the boring goyish girl Rowena. This was *intolerable* to William

Makepeace Thackeray, author of *Vanity Fair* and an *Ivan-hoe* superfan. Not only did he name his own book's heroine Rebecca, he actually wrote a fanfic in which Rowena—who he called "that icy, faultless, prim, niminy-piminy" and "that vapid, flaxen-headed creature, who is in my humble opinion, unworthy of Ivanhoe"—turns into an anti-Semitic shrew who totally *knows* Ivanhoe should've ended up with Rebecca.)

Gratz's noble goal was to educate and civilize the less fortunate. Her school provided food and clothing for poor children, and her lessons stressed morality and philosophy as much as textual study. The students used Christian texts, because there weren't any kid-friendly Jewish texts written in English. Gratz was emphatic about teaching in English, as the goal of her school was to nurture not just little Jews, but little Americans.

Sunday schools caught on like wildfire. They opened all over the Eastern Seaboard. They were designed to be fun—Gratz handed out oranges and pretzels, which to a poor kid were a big honking deal. Thousands of families enrolled. By the turn of the twentieth century, the historian Jacob Rader Marcus wrote, Sunday schools were "America's most important Jewish acculturational agency." And they were designed and run largely by women.

## FIGHTING BACK AGAINST BAD-VALUES EDUCATION

Now that most Jews are living in a peculiar time in history and high-falutin' income bracket, we have to put our child-rearing imprint on a culture of competitive madness that's more about *winning* than about *learning*. The challenge now is to keep traditional Jewish mothering values of emphasizing questioning and dialogue. It's to avoid getting swept up in the hyperfocus of grabbing the brass ring (the right nursery school, the "best" elementary school, the perfect extracurriculars to get into the best-as-graded-by-*U.S.-News-and-World-Report* college) so you can go around again, on to the next grab. Remember that we Jews have been successful because we *haven't* followed the path set up for more privileged folks. We've raised kids to be challengers of authority and independent thinkers, not dutiful bubble-filler-inners. That's what has served us well in a wide variety of settings and cultures. As the Greek philosopher Plutarch (not a Jew) put it, "The correct analogy for the mind is not a vessel that needs filling, but wood that needs igniting."

In 2015, our friends at Harvard's Making Caring Common Project released a report, "Turning the Tide," with findings endorsed by fifty colleges nationwide. It said that the high-stress academic environment many kids labor under is bad for them, and bad for the world. The colleges that signed on to the report's findings urged students to lead more balanced lives, with more emphasis on kindness and long-term service and less on résumé-padding, test-taking, and participating in a zillion extracurriculars. The dean of undergraduate admissions at Yale told the nonprofit education site The Seventy Four, "We want students who have achieved in and out of the classroom, but we're also looking for things that are harder to quantify: Authentic intellectual engagement, a concern for others and the common good, a sense of community building amongst students and peers." Next year's Yale admissions form includes a question asking students about their contributions to family, community, or the public good.

The report recommends decreasing emphasis on standardized testing—including the SAT and ACT, urges students to do some form of service for its own sake and not to game the system, stresses the importance of helping out at home, and urges quality of extracurricular activities over quantity. It also asks kids and families to look at a variety of schools to find the one that fits them best, even if it's not necessarily a prestigious ooh-la-la school.

## NO SCHOOL CAN DO EVERYTHING— THAT'S WHERE PARENTS COME IN

I went to a Jewish day school from kindergarten through eighth grade. An alternative to Sunday school plus secular school, Jewish day schools (where secular education and religious education happen under the same roof) have enrolled, as children, 23 percent of current Jewish adults. My school was run by Orthodox Jews; my family wasn't Orthodox, but my mom really wanted me and my brother to have a hard-core Jewish education, and at the time, it was the only game in town. My school's values didn't always dovetail with my family's. It was not, shall we say, a feminist place. So my mom diligently let me know that there are different perspectives on women's roles in religious life and outside the home, different ways to practice Judaism, different attitudes toward the interplay of religious life and contemporary culture.

I made a conscious choice to send my own kids to a

diverse public school instead of Jewish day school. (I also let them eat pork sausage. This is why some readers of *Tablet*, the Jewish magazine I write for, have accused me of being personally responsible for the impending doom of the Jewish people.) I agonized about this decision, school not bacon, even though like many American Jews, we couldn't have afforded Jewish day school for two kids anyway. I loved the feeling of being transported by prayer; I loved the ancient melodies we learned; I had pride about studying Jewish texts; I wished my kids could be as fluent in Hebrew as I was. My kids go to Sunday school (ours is held on Mondays and Wednesdays after secular school; go figure) and they've never even been taught Hebrew script. That's what actual Hebrew speakers write in; print is only for street signs, novels, and Torahs. I watch my children painstakingly block-printing every letter as if they're writing ransom notes. It pains me.

But I think my kids have gained more than they've lost by going to secular public schools. It delights me that my kids' world is broader and more diverse than mine. I did not have a conversation with a black person who was not cleaning my house until I was thirteen years old. I did not know, as a small child, that bad things happened to people who weren't Jewish. I still have little sense of historicity; as a child I learned that all Torah stories were literally true, and I have no idea what can be historically proven or what century it happened in. I can pray in rapid-fire Hebrew—it's almost Pavlovian at this point—but I don't know who wrote given prayers, or when.

My school gave me a narrow, self-absorbed view of the world. You cannot raise a kid to become a decent human being—a mensch—unless you teach them empathy. Narcissism doesn't allow room for anyone's experience of the world but one's own. I hope that parents who choose parochial schools of all flavors—Jewish, Christian, Muslim—make sure their kids are learning to appreciate difference. Scrap that. I hope they're teaching their kids about the connected sameness of all people; our differences add interest and color, but shouldn't be a cause of separation or division.

If the school doesn't do the job (and some schools do!), parents need to pick up the slack . . . the way my mom did. A kid can become an open-minded person and a creative thinker no matter what kind of school they attend: public, private, parochial. This whole book is about what parents can do to support, reinforce, and in some ways supersede the kind of messages and learning a kid gets in the classroom.

"One size fits all is an incomplete sentence," as we say in the community of fat girls who like cute clothes. This is true of education as well as skirts. Way back in the day, *Menorat HaOr* quoted one rabbi, Rava, saying, "If there are two teachers, one more learned but less attentive to the children, the other less learned but more attentive, the more learned one is appointed. The children's errors will eventually disappear of their own accord." And then it quoted Rabbi Dimi, disagreeing with Rava: "The one who is more attentive is appointed, because once an error has been absorbed it cannot be eradicated." If this book teaches you anything, I hope that it's that experts—secular ones as well as Jewish ones—do not agree on anything, so you might as well listen to your own instincts and do your own research.

We all want a great education for our kids, whether we're Jewish or not. The question is what constitutes a great education. I'd argue that the single most important choice you can make is finding a school that doesn't just pay lip service to notions of citizenship, kindness, and collaboration. Sadly, a lot of parents think of ethics as a luxury, the equivalent of an optional aftermarket accessory for a car. Nope. Ethics are not analogous to butt-warming leather seat technology. A few years ago, *New York* magazine ran a story entitled "Is Ethical Parenting Possible?" and I wanted to punch someone in the eye. It is more important that your child learn about cooperation, kindness, conscientiousness, self-control, perseverance, and curiosity than it is that they get into Harvard. (I say this as someone who went to Harvard.)

Pay attention, too, to the unspoken messages your kids may get in their school. My education-professor mom taught me the term "hidden curriculum," which means lessons that aren't articulated at school, but that are woven into the school's culture and teachings. At many schools, the hidden curriculum tells kids to be competitive little freaks . . . and if that means cheating on a test, well, you gotta do what you gotta do. Schools may have a hidden curriculum full of subterranean lessons in racism and sexism and bullying. But a hidden curriculum can be wonderful too, if the message inextricably wound into the moral fabric of the school is: Treat everyone with respect; everyone has something to learn from someone else; every kid has gifts and skills, and cooperation and supportive behavior are more important than being at the highest reading level. I urge you as a parent to be familiar with all the lessons your kid is learning in the school building, not just the lessons in their books. If the school is not a compassionate and supportive place, that's way more important to address with the principal than the fact that your kid got a B- on a test.

The Making Caring Common Project found that there's huge variation among schools in terms of how much they foster "cultures of caring." Does your kid's school promote kindness? A school can be both kind and rigorous, but everyone—teachers, administrators, parents, students— needs to work to create this culture. As my mom—my education mentor!—put in one of her books, "To be moral one must live in a moral community, a community that cares about the well-being of all of its members. A moral community demands that teachers and parents become role models for the young."

## TEACH YOUR KID THAT EVERYONE HAS CHALLENGES AND GIFTS

"Ours is a nation of immigrants," wrote Julia Richman (1855–1912), the first woman superintendent of schools in New York City. "The citizen voter of today was yesterday an immigrant child. Tomorrow he may be a political leader. Between the alien of today and the citizen of tomorrow stands the school, and upon the influence exerted by the school depends the kind of citizen the immigrant will become."

Richman was a wealthy uptown Jew who made a conscious choice to work on the immigrant Lower East Side, home to underperforming schools and huddled masses yearning to breathe free. You might think that non-native-English-speaking kids in mediocre schools would be the ones most in need of drills and rote memorization, but this wasn't Richman's view. She believed that early childhood education was best conveyed through experience, nature, and stories. "What do these babies care about Adam and Eve, or the order of creation?" she wrote in 1896. "Introduce them to the wonders of plant and animal life. *Show them God* in the bursting seed, in the budding flower, in the bird-producing egg, the glorious sunshine." Amen, Julia. This is exactly what today's progressive educators say our overscheduled, overtested kids actually need. Kids need free time to play outside, and opportunities for unstructured free play and discovery. Bring on the jungle gym; bring out the building blocks.

And bring on the values that show kids that everyone has challenges—academic, behavioral, social. This is something my kids' elementary school, which had mixed-age classrooms that combined special education and general education students, taught very well. When Josie was in fourth grade, I idly called a character in *The Tale of Despereaux,* the book we were reading at bedtime, "stupid."

Josie gasped. "You said the s-word!"

"But Mig *is* stupid!" I replied.

"She doesn't get to go to school, her dad sold her as a slave, she keeps getting her ears clouted, and she doesn't have books!" Josie answered. "She doesn't have the opportunity to do her best work!"

You may roll your eyes at the edu-jargon my kid has picked up, but the values behind it are rock-solid: Don't be a snot. When Jo was six, we were on vacation with my family; Josie kept trying to teach Maxie and our younger cousin Lev how to play ring-around-the-rosy. Lev was so smitten with Josie he just kept beaming at her and forgetting to fall down. Max was so eager to fall down she'd go toppling over as soon as we'd finished singing the first two bars of the song. Josie kept trying to clarify to the toddlers how the game was supposed to work, but it didn't take. Finally she sighed and suggested, "Maybe now would be a good time for us to break into smaller groups." (On the same trip, she asked of Lev, "Is he a good swimmer, or a learner?")

As it turned out, when Maxie started school, she had some challenges with balance, speech, sensory issues, and motor coordination. She got an Individualized Education Program (a legal document entitling a kid to extra help under the Individuals with Disabilities Education Act) that entitled her to occupational therapy at school. I was so grateful to be at a public school that supported both my conventionally high-achieving older kid and my quirkier younger one. I'm pretty confident that if my kids were in private school, Maxie would have had a harder time, and I'd have paid through the schnoz for the wonderful services she got for free. Maxie adored Mallory, her occupational therapist, who worked with her on not flopping all over the floor and into other kids' personal space, all while making it feel like play. Max never felt shamed for needing extra help. Mallory showed my husband and me how to pull and compress Max's joints and gave us a little brush to move over her skin, echoing a sensory integration technique she performed in school. Maxie loved these treatments, sighing, "It's like a spa day!" (She had never been to a spa. She was five. I think she heard about them on *Phineas and Ferb*.) Today, she has bloomed into a hilarious, book-devouring kid who still has a delightfully off-center sensibility. I will be forever grateful to her elementary school for helping her and keeping her sense of self intact.

I realize that I was blessed to find a school that worked for two very different learners. Regardless of your own kid's predilections and gifts and difficulties, you should consider the words of the eighteenth-century Hasid rabbi Zusya: "In the world to come, they will not ask me, 'Why were you not Moses?' They will ask me, 'Why were you not Zusya?'" That's what we should expect of our children: not that they'll all be rock stars, but that they all do their best work. We can't all be Albert Einstein or Bette Midler, but we can all do our damnedest to be our best selves.

To sum up: Talking seriously with and reading to your kids, enjoying reading yourself, taking kids to free concerts and puppet shows and plays, walking through a variety of neighborhoods and getting ice cream, visiting old houses of worship and museums, doing good works and taking care of pets are all vital parts of education. No school, no matter how prestigious, teaches everything. You, the parent, are your child's primary educator.

## 𝒪𝒪 Mamaleh Methodology

1. Remember that education doesn't only happen in school. Talk with kids about the news, culture, sports, and politics. Talk, talk, talk. More on that in the next chapter.

2. Encourage your child and your child's school to chill out about homework and standardized testing. Do I really need to say more here?

3. Remember to ask, "What questions did you ask today?"

4. READ. See number two.

## Chapter 7

# Tell Stories

If Grandma had wheels, she'd be a wagon.

—*Yiddish proverb*

Storytelling has literally been lifesaving for our people. Author Neil Gaiman has talked about his cousin Helen, who survived the Warsaw Ghetto during World War II. "At that point in time, books were illegal and there was a death sentence for anyone found possessing one," he said in an interview with the U.N. Refugee Agency. "However, Helen had a Polish translation of *Gone with the Wind,* and she kept it hidden behind a loose brick in the wall. She would stay up late every night reading so that when the girls came in the next day she could tell them what had happened in the chapters she had read the previous night, and just for that hour these girls got out of the Warsaw Ghetto." He concluded, "This made me realize that fiction is not just escapism, it can actually be escape. And it's worth dying for."

Narratives are how we form identity. Family stories and religious stories, as well as the books we have at home, tell kids who they are, where they're from, and what we hope they'll value. Everything can be an opportunity for a story: making dinner, events in the news, taking your kids to vote, even buying a toothbrush. (Again I remind you: *horim*, parents, and *morim*, teachers, come from the same Hebrew root.)

Stories encourage follow-up questions. They teach morality; they invite debate. A huge part of good parenting is encouraging the *why*s, even though hearing a ton of "why" can make you want to put out your own eye with a spork. When Josie was six, she exploded at Maxie, then three: "*Why, why, why!* I'm sick of you saying '*why*'! Stop saying '*why*' all the time!" In my Infinitely Patient Mother voice, I said, "Josie, all little kids say 'why' all the time. *You* said 'why' all the time." "I *know*," Josie replied. "But the difference is that I didn't have to *listen* to it!"

Jews have always been all about the why. Why did God ask Abraham to sacrifice his only son? Why do bad things happen to good people? Why aren't Jews allowed to eat pork? (We're not? Uh-oh.) (That was a Woody Allen joke.)

Our oral tradition is vast and lively. In addition to all the arguing, we have lots of prayers to memorize, lots of singing, lots of chanting. Our written tradition really didn't start until after 70 CE, when Jews were scattered to the winds, when we weren't all in each other's faces all the time, and perhaps when Christianity began to pick up steam and Jews started to realize they'd better get their stuff codified before it got snuffed out, drowned out, or mixed in with other people's stories.

Linguist Deborah Tannen, in her studies of Jewish conversational patterns, says that Jews tend to tell more stories in conversation, tell them dramatically, and focus on the emotional experience of a story. Not only does this hamminess make for engaging, lively storytelling, but it also teaches kids to identify with and question varying points of view.

Jewish mothers have always been the storytellers-in-chief. A Yiddish proverb says, "One mother achieves more than a hundred teachers." Whether we're outside-work moms or at-home-most-of-the-time moms, we're usually the ones conveying values, setting expectations of behavior, nurturing the curiosity and love of learning and confidence and general chutzpah that together have allowed Jews to become leaders in an immense number of fields, across strata of political thought and throughout arts and sciences. I'd argue that the storytelling is a big part of the why. Another Yiddish proverb (yes, another one, shut up) says, "The entire world rests on the tip of the tongue." The spoken word has the power to transport, entertain, encourage dreams, crush hopes, elucidate, educate, and enlighten.

## HOW STORIES MAKE US SMARTER

All kinds of stuff happen in the brain when we hear a story. MRIs have shown that not only do the parts of the brain that work on language processing light up, but all the areas of the brain that we'd need if the story were real are activated too. For instance, if a storyteller talks about the delicious smell of chicken soup simmering on the stove, the listener's olfactory cortex is engaged. If the story involves racing through snowy woods, blood flow increases to the listener's motor cortex, the part of the brain that initiates voluntary muscle activity.

Sharing a narrative not only engages different parts of the brain, but also builds connections between the tale teller and listener. Uri Hasson of Princeton's Neuroscience Institute has shown that during a storytelling session, the speaker and the listeners experience very similar brain activity. (Princeton calls it a "mind meld," which I will allow, since Mr. Spock is a cool geek.)

The notion that stories have brain-boosting power is echoed by Raymond Mar, a psychologist at York University in Canada. He analyzed 86 MRI studies and found that stories help us understand other people better. When we identify with characters' struggles and triumphs and adventures and desires, we gain insight into actual human behavior. Mar also found that there's a lot of overlap in the areas of the brain that interpret stories and the areas that assist us in interactions with other people. So stories increase kids' social savvy and empathy. Be a storyteller and build a storyteller . . . and help human beings connect.

## START STORYTELLING EARLY

Research shows that the number of different words a baby hears each day is the single most important predictor of school success and social competence. A groundbreaking 2003 study from the University of Kansas found that poor kids tend to hear thirty million fewer words than wealthier kids by the time they're three years old . . . and the overwhelming number of words three-year-olds use are derived from parents' and caregivers' vocabularies. The study also found that kids' speech patterns were very close to those of their parents and caregivers, which reminds me of three-year-old Maxie's response to Josie whining about me being unfair: "Oh, hush, Josie, you know she's just *lovely* to you."

By the time kids are three, the number of words they hear is closely correlated to how well they perform a decade later in school, in terms of vocabulary, language development, and reading comprehension. Of course, there's a correlation/causation question here: Poor kids experience a ton of unfairness and challenges, so how do we know it's the talk that makes the difference? We don't. But I can tell you that Jews have often historically been poor, and we have always talked a blue streak. So talk.

Everyone has a story. One of the great delights of living on the Lower East Side is getting to buy breakfast on Sundays at Russ and Daughters, the delightful historic smoked-fish emporium. Not only is the fish transcendent (and not only do I feel a connection to my forebears when I take a numbered paper tag from the tag-dispensing machine), but I also get to have epic random conversations in the endless line. There are Japanese tourists, Williamsburg hipsters, elderly Long Island matrons, and the occasional lunatic. They come with tales of the band they heard last night, of the first time they had herring, of their grandmothers shopping at this very store, of political intrigue, of finding a parking spot. I get very excited whenever anyone wants to *kibitz*. (That means chat.) My mother-in-law once accompanied me on a lox-buying expedition, which usually means waiting for at least twenty minutes; as we left, she clucked at me, "You really will talk to *anyone!*" Yes. I will. This is the nicest insult-compliment I have ever gotten.

## STORYTELLING AT THE TABLE

Our tradition is full of stories. Genesis is the part of the Torah with the best ones: You get your Adam and Eve, Cain and Abel, Noah's Ark, the Tower of Babel, the destruction of Sodom and Gomorrah, Abraham's near sacrifice of Isaac, Jacob and Esau, Joseph and his fabulous coat and his adventures in Egypt. These minimalist narratives tell primal tales of love, hatred, jealousy, sibling rivalry, fury, revenge, and allow the storyteller to put in all kinds of extra resonances, dialogue, hypotheses, details. (That's a lot of what the Talmud does—it elaborates on questions raised by the Torah.) Jewish children have grown up with these stories for generations.

Any kind of sustained narrative can be an opportunity for engagement. No need to go far out of your way, economically or emotionally, to indulge your kid. No need to strive to be intellectual or deep in your storytelling. It's when you're grimly trying to force a kid to listen and learn IMPORTANT THINGS, regardless of his or her level of interest, that the kid will see through you like they have X-ray vision and you are Lois Lane's underwear.

One advocate of clever storytelling was our pal Grace Aguilar, the nineteenth-century British writer we discussed earlier. She wrote that *doing* stuff with kids to encourage their sense of wonder was more important than textual study. She encouraged Jewish mothers to compose their own prayers with their children, and to paraphrase biblical teachings in their own words rather than sticking to the script. She wrote of "the religion of the heart"—that is, not just rules and regulations, but the love of narrative, good feelings, and a sense of agency about one's own faith. "To speak of God, to teach the child his will, to instill his love into the infant heart, should never be looked on as a daily task, nor associated with all the dreaded paraphernalia of books and lessons," she wrote. In other words, make it fun.

Aguilar's mother provided most of her Jewish education until she was twelve (which was when Grace wrote her first complete work, a play—now tragically lost—about a Swedish king). Then her father fell ill with tuberculosis. While he was home convalescing, he shared with his daughter the oral history of his ancestors, Sephardic crypto-Jews (secret Jews) who'd been forced to convert to Catholicism in the fourteenth or fifteenth century. These were exciting stories—and there are still lots of historically grounded children's books about today's descendants of forced converts who continue their Jewish rituals behind closed doors, sometimes not even knowing why. In Aguilar's case, her father's stories served as fodder for her historical romance writing.

Aguilar herself never had children. Her health was always fragile, and she died of a bone disease at thirty-one. But she left a lasting legacy—not just in her insistence on the vital role of mothers in Jewish storytelling and education of their own children, but also in the New York Public Library system. In 1886, the Aguilar Free Library Society in New York City was established, honoring its namesake's work by circulating literature in Jewish neighborhoods. Today, one of the oldest divisions in New York's library system is the Grace Aguilar branch on East 110th Street. Aguilar's writings went on to influence Julia Richman, who used them to shape the New York City public school system in the late nineteenth century and early twentieth century.

## BE A BETTER STORYTELLER

Let's talk a bit more about the oral tradition before we move on to books. There are a million stories in the naked city, and also during diaper changes, in the bath, at bedtime, and during cuddle time. I remember the leader of my new moms' group telling us simply to narrate our activities. When babies are really little, she said, don't worry about stimulating their tiny brains or Baby Einsteining them; just talk as you go about your day. "Remember that for a baby, a trip to the vegetable crisper is an exciting journey!" she used to say.

As you get more practice you become a better storyteller. This is convenient, because as kids get older, they understand more complicated stories. Again, anything can become a story; it needn't be rarified and highfalutin'. In our family, something Maxie said several years ago has passed into legend. When she was around four, she and Josie found my sister-in-law Ellen's childhood diary at my mother-in-law's house. Maxie ran downstairs and excitedly told Grandma, "We found Auntie Ellen's old diarrhea! But it was locked so we couldn't read it!" Then she paused and added reflectively, "Even if the diarrhea WAS unlocked I couldn't read it. Because I don't know how to read!" (See, more reasons to encourage literacy.)

We get a lot of mileage out of stories from when our kids were little, and kids love hearing stories about when you were little. Holidays, too, come with their own sets of stories. In my house, we try to have Shabbat dinner every Friday night. Shabbat is a chance for a busy family to regroup, to focus on good food and time together, to engage in a little ritual (candle lighting, blessings over wine and bread) and a chance to catch up on everyone's stories.

But I have to be honest. For us, Shabbat is not always a lovely respite. I try to pick up a challah, but sometimes I just thaw one of those parboiled sourdough loaves from FreshDirect. I used to say (and may have even written in a column or two) that I want Shabbat to be the one night a week when we all always stay home and go electronics-free and bond. But this is ideal-world me speaking. In the real world, sometimes there's an awesome Loser's Lounge tribute to the music of Bryan Ferry and Brian Eno, and Friday night is the only night Jonathan and I can go. Sometimes Friday night is the best time for us all to watch that week's episode of *Top Chef*. Before I had kids I thought Shabbat would be sacrosanct, but now I occasionally let my non-theoretical children go to sleepovers on Friday night. I am as conflicted and in-two-worlds as most moms.

But ambivalence can lead to productive talks with kids about identity and ethical dilemmas. How was my Shabbat as a child different from the Shabbat we have now? Why do I sometimes insist we not read at the table and sometimes let it go? How do we form religious identity in a world in which both my kids are in public school (but go to Hebrew school and Jewish camps) and we don't have any living connection to the old country (though we do have stories about family history and frequent platters of historically important and tasty smoked fish)?

I may not always be my best self on Shabbat, but I have to say I am excellent at Passover. (Conveniently, it only comes once a year instead of fifty-two times.) It helps that Passover comes with its own amazing narrative: Moses leading the people of Israel out of slavery in Egypt. There are pyramids, chariots, plagues, a mad escape, a giant killer wave. The Haggadah—the text we read at the Passover Seder—actually directs us to make the story of the Exodus so immediate, it should feel as if we, not our ancestors, are fleeing the Egyptians. *The story itself tells us to tell a good story.* And yes, storytelling can be just that transporting.

I create a supplement to the traditional Haggadah every year. When my kids were tiny, our Seder was short and consisted mostly of songs in English (like "Let My People Go" and "Frogs"); as they've aged, it's gotten longer, more of it is in Hebrew, and I add new poems and songs. When there are a bunch of little kids in attendance, we have a dance interlude mid-Seder, to the tune of "Sisters Are Doing It for Themselves," so that everyone can get their ya-yas out while simultaneously paying tribute to Moses's sister Miriam, who led the Israelite women in singing and dancing at the Red Sea. The adults wave a blue sheet up and down to symbolize the sea, and the kids run crazily under it and back out, shaking their groove thing to Annie Lenox and Aretha. Josie and Maxie contribute to the storytelling, creating illustrations for the Haggadah supplement, which I photocopy *in color,* which is very expensive so they know how much I love them. When we open the box of Passover supplies, we see all the previous years' drawings and note the way their art has changed over time. One year the kids wrote Passover Mad Libs. Once they made an Egyptian centerpiece (complete with charioteers and baby Moses in a basket) out of LEGO and Playmobil.

The story of Passover lends itself beautifully to broader stories about liberation. One year when there was a domestic-workers'-rights bill in the New York State Senate, we talked at our Seder about what life is like for less advantaged people now, and how passage of that law would change things—or if indeed it would—for workers and their employers. One year we read Maya Angelou's poem "Caged Bird" and talked about what it meant. One year we talked about bullying, and how standing up to a friend who's being a schmuck to someone else can be even harder than standing up to an enemy like Pharaoh. We've talked about how the very configuration of the Seder table has changed over the years: We have non-Jewish friends join us, and we have an orange on the Seder plate, a tribute to a famous apocryphal story about a rabbi once saying, "A woman belongs on the pulpit the way an orange belongs on a Seder plate!" The orange stands for the women and LGBT Jews whose stories haven't been told enough in Jewish history. (And it was professor Susannah Heschel's idea.)

You don't need to host a Seder to think about how storytelling and family history can become an integral part of your dinner plans. Talk about your own childhood; talk about where your parents came from; talk about how different family members have different politics.

## STORYTELLING PRESERVES FAMILY HISTORY

I always tell the kids of my own parents' dueling Seders: My dad—who died when I was pregnant with Maxie, when Josie was almost three—led a very traditional Seder. My brother and I called it the *huminah-huminah* Seder, after the sound of droning in rapid-fire, incomprehensible Hebrew. The next night, my mom would lead a supercreative Seder involving lots of English, paper-bag theatricals, a mock trial of Pharaoh. By telling my kids about my parents' Seders,

I share the message that Judaism is ever-evolving; I share something of my own childhood; I offer a glimpse of *Zayde,* the grandfather they never knew.

For my kids, stories and pictures are the only way to know *Zayde,* a man I found maddening and wonderful in equal measure. Josie says, "I think I remember sharing a frozen lemonade with him, and I think I remember flying kites?" But then she says that maybe she only *thinks* she remembers because the photos of those times hang on the door of the room she shares with Max. Or maybe she only *thinks* she remembers because she's heard the stories from me so many times. But does it matter? Does it make a difference if her memories are real if they're . . . well, true? Stories don't bring my dad back. But they make me feel a little less bitter that my children won't know him, because my kids feel that they do. That's the power of stories—he's alive to them, a little bit. Not enough. But life's not fair. (Stories can say that, too. Kids can take it.) To quote the musical *Hamilton,* "Who lives, who dies, who tells your story?"

Now that Josie's a teenager (i.e., not a morning person), I tell her about the time my father made good on his threat to pour a cup of water on my head if I wouldn't get out of bed and get ready for school. I tell Maxie, who likes to walk around the neighborhood with me on errands, about the special trips I went on with my dad when I was her age; he'd take me to a liquor store in Pawtucket, where he'd stock up on Campari and Chilean red wine with a little plastic bull around the neck of the bottle (I got to keep the bull) and buy me a faintly illicit Slim Jim, which we weren't allowed to eat in our kosher home, but which we could plead *nolo contendere* to when outside the house.

My father was a great storyteller. He was a blogger

before we had the word *blog*. He had a website on which he told stories of his own childhood, reviewed great restaurant meals, shared prank letters he wrote to companies, told stories of our Seders and other Jewish holidays, *kvell*ed about my brother's and my weddings. After he died, my husband sweetly moved it to our own server, where it lives in perpetuity. (It's at www.farklempt.com, if you want to look. *Farklempt* is Yiddish for "all choked up," which Dad got whenever he talked about his loved ones. He also had a tendency to break into loud renditions of "Sunrise, Sunset." Naturally, this mortified me.)

Dad wrote a lot on his website about baby Josie. Not long ago, I had the surreal experience of having her plunk herself down on my lap (which happens rarely now) to read what my father had written about her. He swore like a sailor in his writing—even about his beloved grandbaby, who he regularly called a fucking genius—and I loved listening to Josie chortle in scandalized pride. He insisted she was a jigsaw puzzle savant, that she could sing all the verses of "Twinkle, Twinkle," and that she was the sweetest toddler on earth. (She wasn't.) What a privilege for her to be able to read his actual words and feel his love—thanks to his own storytelling.

Another Yiddish proverb: "Only love gives us the taste of eternity."

## READ TO YOUR KIDS
## FOR AS LONG AS THEY'LL LET YOU

Jews as a group have been literate perhaps as far back as the tenth century BCE. Our stories were some of the few things we could carry with us as we got kicked out of Carthage, Alexandria, the Visigoth Empire, Mainz, France, Germany, Upper Bavaria, England, Switzerland, Saxony, Hungary, Belgium, Slovakia, Italy, Spain, Sicily, Lithuania, Portugal, Pia, Austria, Ukraine, and Poland. (Some of those countries let us come back, then booted us again. Much like Lucy yanking the football away from Charlie Brown, only with more death.)

I don't necessarily think Jews are smarter than other groups. Maybe we just read more. If I actually believed that Jews were inherently brainier than other people due to our awesome Jewy genes, I would not be writing a book telling you that Jewish parenting is worth emulating. Also, I would be insufferable.

Research shows that hearing stories aloud builds language skills that make learning to read on one's own easier and more pleasurable. Hearing a book over and over—while deeply annoying for the parent who has to read that book— helps kids gain comprehension, reinforces neural connections, and assists with memory, vocabulary, and sequencing. Being read to leads to greater interest in books, and greater interest in books leads to more school success and more creative thinking. You have all my sympathy if you're reading *Barnyard Dance* for the seven zillionth time, but welcome to parenthood. We've all been there. Suck it up. Repetition is a vital developmental stage, even if it makes you want to climb down that ladder that the *Love You Forever* mom left at her son's window (the freak) and flee into the night.

Read to kids not because reading is a tool to winning the Race to the Top or conquering the Common Core, but because it's fun, because school is not enough, because books give kids the sense of the bigness of the universe and all the possibilities their future holds. The world changes so fast now; learning *things* isn't enough; to be able to think on their feet, as Jews have done throughout history, you have to learn *how* to think. You have to want to challenge yourself and want to explore.

George Saunders, a writer I adore, once said, "A minute spent reading to your kids now will repay itself a million-fold later, not only because they love you for reading to them, but also because, years later, when they're miles away, those quiet evenings, when you were tucked in with them, everything quiet but the sound of the page-turns, will seem to you, I promise, sacred."

I've read that sentence a hundred times and it still makes me weepy.

Today, when test-score-obsessed schools are teaching "texts" instead of books, teaching semi-coherent snippets instead of sustained stories, it's even more important to encourage older kids to explore stories and books. Professor Mar has done work showing that readers of fiction tend to be more empathetic and better at making inferences than those who aren't big fans. But whatever your kid will read—online news, magazines, fanfiction, graphic novels, terrible emo poetry—is worth reading. From around age four on, Josie disliked books with nonhuman protagonists. (Except Wilbur from *Charlotte's Web*. And thank goodness. Because if you don't love Wilbur, I don't want to know you.) Maxie rejected all books with pretty pastel art; she preferred bolder, cartoonier illustrations. If a book isn't working for your kids, for God's sake give up and try something else.

## A BRIEF JEWISH INTERLUDE ABOUT
## JEWISH CHILDREN'S LITERATURE

Early Jewish children's books, like children's books in general, tended to be didactic, humorless, and spinachy. But K'tonton, created by Sadie Rose Weilerstein, was anything but. "The Jewish Tom Thumb" made his first appearance in a magazine story in 1930; a book, *The Adventures of K'tonton,* followed in 1935. K'tonton (which literally is a contraction of the Hebrew for "little-little") was a good little thumbling, but like Curious George, his inquisitiveness often got him into trouble. He fell into a vat of fish and rode his mom's chopping knife like a bucking bronco! He was carried away on a runaway dreidel. Adventure!

The book was so appealing because kids love teeny things. And because K'tonton was a desperately wanted baby (his mom had wished for a child so hard, she said she wouldn't have cared if he were no bigger than a thumb)—what reader wouldn't crave feeling so wanted? K'tonton was a savvy mix of Jewish and American, an early example of the balancing act contemporary non-Orthodox Jews have to manage all the time.

The books offer lots of onomatopoeia and repetition, and no dry-as-dust moral lectures. Stories need to stand on their own *as stories.* That's something we need to remember as we help our kids choose developmentally appropriate books that will make them want to keep reading.

I loved K'tonton when I was five or six, but by the time I was seven or eight, it was all about the *All-of-a-Kind Family* books. These were stories—still beloved today by Jews and non-Jews alike (as opposed to K'tonton, who never really broke out of the literary *shtetl*) about a big, poor Jewish family living in a Lower East Side tenement at the beginning of the twentieth century. The first book in the series—introducing us to sisters Ella, Henny, Sarah, Charlotte, and Gertie—came out in 1951; it has aged really, really well. All-of-a-Kind books are full of food (chocolate babies, whatever they were, broken cookies, pickles, chickpeas in paper cones) and mischief and warm family times (and scary disciplinary stories too, like that time Sarah refused to eat her soup and it was served to her for the next three meals until she caved and ate a bite). If you don't know them, stop reading this right now and go get them for yourself or your spawn.

These books speak to me in part because they reflect my own cultural history. I encourage you to explore children's books that come from your own family background, whatever it is. But I also think it's important that kids read books about other kids who aren't much like them. That's how we connect with one another; that's how we build bridges; that's how we become more empathetic people.

## HELP KIDS FIND THEIR LITERARY SWEET SPOT

Maxie took her sweet time reading independently. She just wasn't interested. But she always loved stories. So I kept reading to her and tried hard (sometimes successfully) not to stress about her unhurriedness to strike out on her own.

Much later, my mom pointed out that my younger daughter is an aural learner, not a visual one. I was worried about her learning the *Ashrei,* a long and wordy Hebrew prayer, in time to recite it at Josie's Bat Mitzvah. I tried teaching her in Hebrew. I tried transliterating. Just when I was ready to back off and suggest she do an easier prayer, my mom suggested singing the *Ashrei* to Max and having her sing it back, phrase by phrase, rather than trying to help her sound out each syllable. You know what? She learned it perfectly, in a matter of days. Someone in the synagogue who didn't know our family asked if the little girl leading the prayer was Israeli. The moral of the story: We all learn differently. Maxie is a listener. Listening to stories is a good way for listeners to learn.

For Maxie, the thing that triggered reading for fun was graphic novels. I think a huge unbroken block of text daunted her, but her eyes liked darting around the lively, busy pages of *Zita the Spacegirl*. She still loves graphic novels, but now she also reads novel-novels. Graphic novels opened the door.

She also loved her Rebecca Rubin American Girl doll, which turned out to be an awesome Trojan Horse for literacy. I loathe the consumerist terror that is the American Girl store, where Kit's bed costs as much as an actual child-sized bed at IKEA and the entire chirpy experience is like roaming a terrifying zombie hellscape. But it turns out that Rebecca and her fellow insanely expensive hunks of plastic have a zillion books associated with them, and a lot of the books are good! One of the Rebecca books is set against the backdrop of the labor strikes of the 1910s and discusses the role of Jewish labor leader Clara Lemlich. (Though *Brave Girl,* a picture book about Clara Lemlich by Michelle Markel, illustrated by Melissa Sweet, is even better.) After reading Rebecca's books, Maxie wanted to read all the other books of all the other historical girls, even though she doesn't have the dolls.

And TV can be your reading-encouragement-buddy, too. Are you aware that there are a zillion *Adventure Time* and *My Little Pony* books? If your spawn is a sports freak, and some athlete they love has written a children's book (which probably sucks, but who cares), check your own taste at the door and pick it up at the library. For a couple of years, Maxie was insane about *Wild Kratts,* a TV show about two dude-bros with annoying vocal mannerisms who teach us about wildlife. Whenever she started monologuing about wild turkey roosting patterns and spiderweb construction, I knew to blame those Kratts. So for the duration of her obsession I got her photography books by Nic Bishop, featuring superfreaky close-ups of spiders and snakes. And we went to the zoo and made up stories about the penguins, and I let her stop and pet every dog on the street and chat with the owners if the owners were willing. If I were a really great mother, I would have arranged for her to volunteer at an animal shelter, but I am merely a good-enough mother (see Chapter 2), and I am tired.

Also, model the behavior you want to see. Be sure your kids see your love of storytelling, narrative-oriented stand-up comedy, reading for pleasure rather than out of some noble obligation to better yourself. (Though I'm still trying to explain why Josie saw *Jurassic Jane Eyre: The Dinosaur Turned Me Lesbian* on my iPad. It was ninety-nine cents, OK? And if Jane Eyre wants to find happiness in an alternate universe in the tiny arms of a loving lady dinosaur, who am I to judge?)

Debate ideas from books at the table. Ask your kid lots of questions about what they're reading, and listen to the answers. And be sneaky. Judy Blume suggests that if we want our kids to read, simply leave books lying around the house and periodically say nonchalantly, "You're not ready to read this yet." (I love her.) Talk about what *you're* reading and why you love it and/or are frustrated by it. Your kid will feel important that you want to talk about literature with him, and you give him the opportunity to build vocabulary and comprehension.

Finally, storytelling is a damn good excuse for cuddling. Not everything has to be about success later in life; there are joys in the here and now, too. Reading, storytelling, making up silly poems together—it's all good.

## ⌒⌒ Mamaleh Methodology

1. **Storytelling doesn't just mean reading!** Listen to storytelling podcasts and radio shows like *The Moth*. Play audiobooks in the car. Retell folktales, fairy tales, urban legends, family lore. Whenever you're telling or reading a story, keep your kid engaged by asking them open-ended questions about the characters or plot, questions the kid can't answer with a yes or no.

2. **If your kid doesn't like to read, don't give up. You haven't found the right book.** Explore different kinds of fiction, poetry, graphic novels, books of world records and kooky facts, profiles of presidents and sports heroes, gross-out science books. Get suggestions from a cool teacher or librarian. If your kid has a learning disability or just isn't into reading on their own, read aloud to them, tell stories and listen to audiobooks together for as long as your kid will let you.

3. **You can't go wrong with funny.** For younger kids, rhyming books are great; they can guess at each rhyme, so there's

built-in suspense. Have no shame when you read aloud: Do accents. Take dramatic pauses. Modulate your voice, raising and lowering it to build narrative momentum. Let your children mock you. My kids always loved when I cried at the end of *Charlotte's Web* or *Mrs. Katz and Tush*. They'd look at each other, snickering, clearly thinking, *Poor Mom, she's daft.*

4. **Dedicate time to reading.** Make it a ritual. Make it part of your day. If your kid is not a sit-still kid, even fifteen minutes of reading a day is better than nothing. And again: You might just not be reading the right book.

5. **Let kids choose their own books.** I've never told my kids they weren't allowed to read something. I learned this from my fabulous mom, who watched me read Deb Putnoi's copy of Judy Blume's *Forever* at a house party when I was nine. Adults were giving her an earful about "letting me" read something so risqué, but she kept replying with variants of "If she has questions, she'll ask me." That was a big lesson for me, and now that I'm a parent, I've exercised veto power only at bedtime, and only once or twice. Because when young Josie got scared she became a hysterical *chaleria* (excessively nervous person: literally "person with cholera") and would fight sleep for days and make us all want to die of exhaustion. (Advice within advice: Let your children read Roald Dahl's *The Witches* only during daylight hours.) And if your kid is reading books you don't approve of—from sexist comic books to poorly written sparkly vampire romance, the worst thing you can do is ban what they love. Talk about why you think certain books are dumb or offensive (or better, let your kid make a book recommendation, actually read the thing, and then discuss the book

together), but don't shame your kid for having different tastes from yours.

6. **Harness peer pressure.** Kids take book recommendations from other kids more seriously than they do recommendations from adults. When Josie went through a sci-fi and fantasy stage, a genre about which I'm clueless, she got book suggestions from her friend Nora.

7. **Get your kid into series books.** They may not be the greatest literature, but they create anticipation and identification with recurring characters. You can always mindlessly borrow or buy the next one in the series, which is a huge relief when you'd rather be thinking about a cocktail than kidlit.

8. **Kids see through "do as I say, not as I do."** Model the behavior you want to see. Invite your kid to sit next to you on the couch as you both read. Keep books out—in baskets, on shelves, and on coffee tables. The way I got Josie to read Harry Potter—which I knew she'd love but which she stubbornly refused to try because she is contrary like her mother—was to take it on vacation, leave it on the coffee table of our rental house, and say absolutely nothing.

9. **Pro Tip: "Two truths and a lie" is a good way to get sullen tweens to tell a story.** Here's the game: At dinner, everyone has to say three things that happened that day, two of which are true and one of which isn't. Then everyone else has to guess which is the lie. It's a sneaky way to get anecdotes out of your kids beyond "How was your day?" *"Fine."*

*Chapter 8*

# Laugh

After the assassination of Tsar Alexander II of Russia, a government official in Ukraine menacingly addressed the local rabbi: "I suppose *you* know who was behind it."

"Ach," the rabbi replied, "I have no idea, but the government's conclusion will be the same as always: they will blame the Jews and the chimney sweeps."

"Why the chimney sweeps?" asked the befuddled official.

"Why the Jews?" responded the rabbi.

—*Old Jewish joke*

The Jews have always been a funny people. Even the Torah has jokes! Genesis tells the story of how Abraham and Sarah urgently wanted children but couldn't conceive. When he's ninety-nine and she's ninety, they learn they're finally going to have a baby. And they crack up. Abraham literally falls on his face, and Sarah says, "I'm worn out and my husband is old; *now* I'm getting this pleasure?" As a result, when they actually do become parents, they call their baby Isaac—Yitzhak in Hebrew—which literally means laughter. (Another Torah joke: After the goyish priests are unable to impel Baal to perform a miracle on demand, Elijah suggests that maybe Baal is off making a poop. Tell this one to a preschooler.)

Humor has long been a Jewish survival strategy. And

157

it's just as effective as a parenting strategy—like Judaism, parenting frequently involves moments of terror and obsessions with food.

Laughter is also a strategy for success in life. When you unleash your kid into the world, that kid's path will be easier if they have a sense of humor. Humor helps win people over to your way of thinking . . . which helps you come out on top, as Jews so frequently have.

## WHAT IS JEWISH HUMOR, SPECIFICALLY, AND WHY SHOULD YOU CARE?

There are specifically Jewish kinds of funniness. As it happens, Jewish humor is often bridge-building humor. It's self-deprecating, it identifies with the downtrodden instead of with the bully, it's frequently about the little guy managing to outwit the thug (David-and-Goliath style). These kinds of jokes work in many settings—they're not so inside-baseball that they're inaccessible to a wider audience, and they're not so threatening or snarky that an outsider can't laugh.

Being funny is an excellent defense mechanism when life is scary and uncertain. As early as the Middle Ages, Jews had humor about schlemiels and schlimazels. (A schlemiel is a guy who always spills his soup. A schlimazel is the guy he spills it on.) The historian of Jewish humor Nathan Ausubel claimed that this kind of sad-sack humor dated back to the times of the emperor Justinian, who made life so difficult for the Jews that all they could do was make fun of themselves and their powerlessness. (Again: Parenting is similar.)

The quintessential example of gentle, self-mocking Jewish humor is the Chelm story. Once, the story goes, some-where in Eastern Europe, there was an entire town of Jewish idiots. That town was called Chelm.

The people of Chelm decided it was time to build a new synagogue. So they sent the strongest men to gather stones for the foundation from atop the nearby mountain. The men carried the stones down on their shoulders. "You fools!" said an older man. "You should have rolled the stones down the mountain! That would have been so much easier!" The strong men agreed. So they carried the stones back up the mountain and rolled them down.

Everyone knows that when you drop a piece of buttered bread, it falls buttered side down. That's life. So when the butcher's wife accidentally dropped a piece of bread and it fell buttered side up, everyone was shocked. The council of elders convened to discuss how this could have occurred. Finally, after seven days of intense study and debate, they announced, "We now understand what happened. The butcher's wife buttered her bread on the wrong side."

The greatest scholar in Chelm was chatting with his wife. "If I were Rothschild, I'd be even richer than he!" he says. "How?" asks his wife. "You'd have the same amount of money." "Ah," says the scholar. "But I'd do a little teaching on the side."

Okay, so these jokes aren't hilarious. But they're gentle, they trigger a little smile, they make us nod in recognition (we've all worked with people who are metaphorically from Chelm, have we not?). Lots of great, funny Jewish writers through history have told Chelm tales: Sholom Aleichem, Y. L. Peretz, Solomon Simon, Isaac Bashevis Singer. Today, you can buy a ton of children's book versions of Chelm tales—including some retold by modern authors like Francine Prose and Eric A. Kimmel and illustrated by picture-book all-stars like Maurice Sendak and Uri Shulevitz. For those who can't stand truly cruel or uncomfortable jokes, sweetly silly humor is a balm. At five or so, Maxie was obsessed with the early reader *There Is a Carrot in My Ear and Other Noodle Tales* by Alvin Schwartz—better known for the *Scary Stories to Tell in the Dark* series—that are essentially updated Chelm tales set in suburbia. As I've mentioned, this kid wasn't ultramotivated to read on her own, but when she was in kindergarten and first grade, she wanted to hear that book over and over at bedtime, and she'd giggle maniacally every time.

We Jews are as known for agile, literate humor as we are for the goofy stuff, of course. From at least the Middle Ages onward, performers called *badhanim* performed at Jewish weddings. They were sort of scholarly court jesters who turned Torah lessons into jokes. In some Orthodox communities, they still perform today. Like a court jester, a *badhan* gets to tease and mock the powerful without sanction. Historically, as we discussed in Chapter 4, Judaism has been comfortable making fun of authority figures, making sure no one gets too self-important simply because they happen to be really rich or really pious. Humor can be a great leveling force as well as a way to address tyranny and unfairness. My brother, Andy, and his husband, Neal, are emphatically not Orthodox, but my brother is fluent in Yiddish, and at their wedding, two female friends dressed up in jester costumes and combined the *badhan* tradition with juggling and Borscht Belt humor. For older guests—most of whom had never attended a gay wedding—here was something traditional and familiar, but with a bit of a spin. Humor can serve as a way to make people comfortable with something they're unenlightened about, something that might otherwise have made them lash out in fear. Jews have used this strategy as they integrated previously WASPy environments, and it still works when you're asking people to move beyond their comfort zone.

But some Jewish humor is superdark, intended more for the in-group than for outsiders. (I see it as the equivalent of the kind of escape fantasies mothers share over a few cocktails on their rare nights out, hysteria- and exhaustion-edged giggle fits that flirt with despair.) A couple of old examples, via Rabbi Joseph Telushkin's *Jewish Humor*:

> Rabbi Altmann and his secretary were sitting in a coffeehouse in Berlin in 1935. "Herr Altmann," said his secretary, "I notice you're reading *Der Stürmer*! I can't understand why. A Nazi libel sheet! Are you some kind of masochist, or, God forbid, a self-hating Jew?"
>
> "On the contrary, Frau Epstein," the rabbi replied. "When I used to read the Jewish papers, all I learned about were pogroms, riots in Palestine, and assimilation in America. But now that I read *Der Stürmer*, I see so much more: that the Jews control all the banks, that we dominate the arts, and that we're on the verge

of taking over the entire world. You know—it makes me feel a lot better!"

A Christian girl was found murdered near a Russian *shtetl*. All the Jewish villagers panicked, fearing a pogrom—a murderous mass riot—as so many poor villages in the Pale of Settlement had experienced so many times before. They gathered silently at the synagogue, awaiting their fate. Suddenly, the rabbi came running in, crying, "Great news! The murdered girl was Jewish!"

You'd have to be careful who you told jokes like this to. You'd have to know they were totally in your corner, that they understood your experiences and worldview. I'd argue that this acidic humor has a place in the world of motherhood—it can be lifesaving. I have a best mom friend to whom I can say absolutely anything—about my kids, my marriage, my work, my fears and anxieties—and know I won't be judged. When you're faced with someone who makes parenting look perfect and easy, with a brilliantly curated stack of smart-person hardcovers at perfect right angles on her midcentury modern coffee table and all her kids' stuff neatly corralled in soothing richly textured organic rattan storage bins in their rooms, it helps to have folks in your life with whom you can share stories about leaving the house unaware of the panty shield stuck to your leg.

Here in America, Jews have long ruled the world of comedy. (We've never owned the media, but we've definitely owned jokes about owning the media.) First we were vaudevillians, then radio comics and Borscht Belt humorists and stand-up comedy stars, as well as funny literary writers and then TV writers and filmmakers. Fanny Brice, Molly Picon, Milton Berle, Sophie Tucker, the Marx Brothers, Neil Simon, Gilda Radner, Gene Wilder, Mel Brooks, Madeline Kahn, Carol Kane, Joan Rivers, Roseanne Barr, Pee-wee Herman, Judd Apatow, the Coen Brothers, Nora Ephron, Nicole Holofcener, Frank Oz, Carl and Rob Reiner, and the writers of a zillion *Simpsons* and *Saturday Night Live* episodes. You have your esteemed-yet-unnerving literary icons like Saul Bellow, Philip Roth, and Joseph Heller, your Norman Mailer and Bernard Malamud.

Basically, for years we had a lock on American comedy, high and low. (As *Cracked* magazine once asked, "Just how unfunny was Noam Chomsky that he was forced into the history business?") Goyish comic Steve Allen suggested in 1981 that 80 percent of the country's leading comics were Jews (and remember, we're only 2 percent of the population). This means that Jewish humor resonates with a lot of people who aren't of the tribe. This could have something to do with our neuroses about food, the intensity of our relationships, our commitment to family, and the inherent drama of our arguing and debating style. It could also have something to do with the socialization strategy of making fun of yourself before someone else can do it.

One might argue that while there were economic reasons for Jewish comedy to take off after World War II— acculturation, suburbanization, the rise of the antihero, auteur theory—there was also an intense emotional need for comic relief. After the Holocaust, laughter was an essential coping mechanism. If we didn't laugh, we'd never stop crying. And then Hitler would have won.

## WHY PARENTS NEED A SENSE OF HUMOR

No one knows that humor is a survival strategy better than a parent.

Parenting small children can be exhausting, mind-numbing, and relentless. Parenting big children can make you feel that you're screwing up constantly. In both cases, laughter is a lifesaver.

There's plenty of evidence that laughter relieves stress. Studies have shown that laughter causes actual physical changes in the body, pulling air into your lungs to stimulate your heart, boosting the endorphins released by your brain to make you feel jazzed and high, spiking and then mellowing out your blood pressure into a feeling of chill good feeling, helping circulation and muscle relaxation. Long-term, regular doses of laughter help improve your immune system response, relieve pain, alleviate depression and anxiety. Jews know from depression and anxiety. And parents of all backgrounds can adapt what Jews know from depression and anxiety to make their own lives with children less depressing and anxiety-making.

One way to cope when you're overwhelmed is to remember times when your children amused you. This keeps you from killing them. I remember one time when Josie was three, watching her do that I-love-you-so-much-my-teeth-are-gritted thing as she patted Maxie's infant hand and began squeezing it with increasing . . . vehemence. I looked at her and said warningly, "Josie . . ." and she blurted out, "I'm feeling AGGRESSED!" I said, "I understand those feelings, but you can't take them out on Maxie. Go squeeze a pillow if you feel aggressive." My husband, watching, said, "Don't pinch Maxie; she doesn't pinch you!" Josie answered: "But I want to make sure I pinch her BEFORE she pinches me!"

Even today, as my children growl and wail and I prepare to yank them apart for the umpteenth time, I tend to find them pretty funny. I'm always thinking of how I'm going to tell these stories of sass and trauma to my mom. (Her "you're getting yours!" comes more often than is strictly necessary.)

If you focus on how funny your kids are, you can see them as people rather than as sources of worry or annoyance or dismay. Once, when I was struggling with Josie's refusal to read Harry Potter (why was I so worked up about her need to read Harry Potter? I was sure she'd love it, but really, what did it matter?), I overheard a fellow seven-year-old trying to sell her on the series.

JOSIE: But what if it's too scary?

ELLIE: It's not that scary.

JOSIE: But I bet there are SOME PARTS that are scary.

ELLIE: Well, for the parts that are scary, you could have your mom read them really fast. Or you could tell your mom to just explain to you what happens.

JOSIE: Or I could just not read it at all. That would be quicker.

I wish I could say I heard this and realized that since Josie's friend couldn't budge her either, and since literary peer pressure can be a force for good and yet here it failed, maybe I needed to *just freaking chill out about Harry Potter.*

But I would be lying. Still, perhaps you as a parent are more evolved. Maybe you would laugh and move on, rightly seeing this conversation as a sign that your kid is their own person and realizing that having a will of iron is beneficial and will help your child as an adult. This is my advice to you that I failed to follow myself. Because I am a good-enough mother, dammit.

Another time, my family was visiting the home of an acquaintance with children. Maxie, then four, asked the hostess politely, "Can I please have a cheese stick?" Internally I beamed at my child's flawless manners. The visitor retrieved a cheese stick from the fridge, and Maxie peeled and ate half. She then looked up at the hostess and said, "I'm lactose intolerant!" The hostess, a look of panic on her face, asked, "Really?" Maxie replied, "Nope."

Was this both odd and rude? Kind of! Was it funny? Totally! The takeaway should be that my kid is her own person with her own idiosyncratic sense of humor, and even at four she liked to mess with people. My parenting challenge is to make sure her humor doesn't turn mean—offbeat is dandy, but cruel is not.

Laughter can not only help you understand your kids better, but also help you teach them. Humor can help you clarify tough concepts, get people (including young ones) to do what you want, prove that you're on the same team as someone else and trying to connect, and help you make a possibly snarky and edgy observation without actually tipping over into nastiness. Physical humor can even help you spark a connection with people who aren't all that verbal or clueful about life yet (peekaboo—the earliest joke!). Not taking yourself or your offspring too seriously is the only way to get through long days with little people. Shoot, with any people.

Laughter can mitigate sorrow, too. On my dad's third *yahrzeit,* the Hebrew anniversary of his death, back when Maxie was two and a half, I felt so sad that he'd never gotten to meet her. Her sense of humor reminds me so much of his, and I know he would have been crazy about her. They missed each other by only two months. Our babysitter Rita, who knew I was feeling melancholy, told me she'd experienced a *sign* that Maxie was truly Zayde's granddaughter and they were connected. She was reading Maxie *Joseph Had a Little Overcoat,* Simms Taback's brilliant and hilarious children's book based on an old Jewish folk song. Joseph has a little overcoat that gets old and worn, so he turns it into a jacket, and then into a vest, and then into a pocket square, and finally into a button. The final line is "It just goes to show, you can always make something out of nothing." Maxie knew the book by heart. Rita read her the ending: "You can always make something out of . . ." and paused to let Maxie fill in the blank. Maxie said, "Poop." (That same day, she also gave a giant sneeze, then screamed, "Aaaaah! I have Bless-You on my shirt!")

My dad loved poop and pee humor. He was a fan of both Werner Herzog and *Porky's.* Seeing Maxie's humor develop as she grows has been such a source of joy (tinged with melancholy) for me. She's Zayde's little girl, even though she never knew him.

Humor can not only help you survive snot and poop and horrid knock-knock jokes, but also create a magic bubble of intimacy and connection, the kind you read about in children's books and don't feel as often as you'd like. Once a few years ago the girls were snuggling in bed with me (Jonathan was already up and making coffee) when my iPhone alarm went off, with its rising and falling ethereal harp sound. I cooed to Josie, then seven, whose eyes were still closed, "Josie, the angels are singing you awake for camp!" Eyes still closed, she muttered, "Shoot them." A child after my own heart.

Laughter can connect you and your kid precisely at the moment when you wonder whether time travel will ever be possible so that you can go back and get your tubes tied. Watch a classic comedy movie together, and out of the corner of your eye, observe your kid giggling, rolling on the floor, losing it. It's a surefire mood-lifter. Humor is a force that unites people of all ages. It can be appreciated at the lowest level and sometimes at a more profound one too. (For instance, the time Maxine, at eight, picked out a donut to take home to Josie, then sighed, saying, "You know, she's going to tell us it's the wrong donut." I agreed, "Whatever kind it is!" Maxie said, "She really needs to relax. She's young! She should smell the roses! Before you know it it'll be time for her Bat Mitzvah and she'll have to take everything seriously, so she should enjoy herself now!")

A nice thing about being a writer is that I have a record of what my kids say, and I can repeat the stories back to my now-much-more-sophisticated children a couple of years later. Then we all get to laugh all over again. It's like having dementia. Even if you're not a writer, you might consider blogging or journaling or keeping a file of e-mails to your mother about the hilarious thing your kid just said or did. (If you don't have a mother, I'm sorry. You can always e-mail me.) They're great to look back on when parenting seems dreary, scary, or onerous.

## HOW TO BE FUNNY WITHOUT BEING A
## SEXIST OR RACIST SCHMUCK

You want to be able to laugh at yourself, and you want to raise a kid who can use humor to maintain perspective, set others at ease, and create a place for themself at a given table. What you don't want is to raise a kid who uses jokes as a cudgel, who uses humor to cause hurt or to deliberately leave others out.

This kind of humor has also had its place in Jewish history. In the years after World War II, when Jews really started to become comedy superstars, other stuff was happening, too. This period coincided with Jews deghettoizing and suburb-ifying, and also with the rise of Jewish mother and Jewish American Princess jokes. As the sociologist Riv-Ellen Prell has pointed out, the American postwar period was when Jewish women began to stay home after having kids and Jewish men started to become educated doctors and lawyers rather than shopkeepers and merchants like their fathers. Suddenly you have all this class anxiety as well as gender anxiety, and mommy issues and the possibility of actually dating outside your religion, and you have young Jewish men being taken seriously as writers and storytellers and performers. Boom.

Much of Jewish men's laughter in that era came at the expense of Jewish women. To a degree, that may be because women loom so large in Jewish identity and tradition. Jewish mothers control ritual life at home, and Judaism is a very home-based-ritual-centric religion: Shabbat candle lighting and dinner, Havdalah (the ceremony that ends Shabbat), eating traditional foods, building a sukkah, having a Passover Seder, Hanukah candle lighting. As we discussed earlier, Jewish mothers have also educated children and made money and kept homes and managed interactions with the non-Jewish world for their husbands. We've had power, and powerful women freak men out. So Jewish mother jokes tend to be about inducing guilt, being selfish, and pressuring children too much to excel.

Q: What's a genius?
A: An average student with a Jewish mother.

Three Jewish mothers are sitting on a park bench.
The first says, "You know how much my son Irving loves me? He bought me a Chagall painting."
The second says, "You think that's something? You've seen my new Mercedes? It's from my son Harry."
The third says, "That's nothing. You know my son Morris? Five times a week he sees a psychiatrist. And what does he talk about the entire time? Me."

These jokes have faded away for several reasons. For one, we Jewish mothers no longer talk with the easy-to-mock rhythms of Yiddish. We sound like everyone else. We've acculturated enough that at least most of us don't brag tackily about possessions (and therapy isn't so exotic anymore). Jews have also integrated so well into the secular world, there's no need for Jewish men to call out The Mother as the personification of The Other. And comedy has moved on—it's not so rimshoty, not so presentational. It's often more intimate and observational and authentic. (It's more like storytelling!)

It's no coincidence that the Jewish American Princess (JAP) joke has also faded. By the time I started college in the mid-'80s, JAP talk was on the way out, and today, most teenagers and twentysomethings are familiar with the phenotype but not the genotype. They know the traits: overly made up, vapid, obsessed with clothes and shopping, uninterested in any sort of intellectual life, perpetually working out but only because she sees her body as an object rather than a source of strength or pleasure. Her funds come from Daddy, and she has no ambition beyond marriage to a rich guy.

Q: What is the only thing a JAP will go down on?
A: The escalator at Neiman Marcus.

Q: What's a JAP's favorite sexual position?
A: Facing Bloomingdale's.

Q: What is a JAP's favorite wine?
A: I wanna go to Floridaaaaaa!

Today, JAP-py has been superseded by "betch" and "basic" and whatever the current word is to insult young women, not specifically tied to religion. Even women who look like the princess stereotype usually expect to enjoy careers and/or families, not to shop all day.

We all need to be wary of the ways humor can be used to stereotype and hurt. Teach your kids to joke inclusively or self-deprecatingly. Teach them not to keep silent when someone else makes a sexist, racist, anti-Semitic, ageist, sizeist, homophobic, or transphobic joke. To be clear, I think almost any subject is fair game for humor. But crappy humor aligns the joke teller and joke listener against a marginalized group instead of in support of them. A rape joke can be hilarious if the sympathy is clearly for the victim rather than the aggressor. Much of Jewish humor involves identifying with those who have less power—these jokes are the ones to emulate.

Today, writers and scholars worry that Jewish humor is dying out. We don't have a Borscht Belt anymore. New Yawk and Yiddishche Mama accents are disappearing. Jews, increasingly, are insiders, who may not be as good at commenting on the status quo or on systemic injustice as outsiders. Jon Stewart has retired, and a world mourned.

But there are still an awful lot of youngish Jewish comedians. There's Lena Dunham, Amy Schumer, Sarah Silverman, Nick Kroll (Solomon Schechter School of Westchester, represent!), Chelsea Handler, Jenny Slate, Jason Segel, Seth Rogen, Paul Rudd, Jack Black, Ophira Eisenberg, Abbi Jacobson, and Ilana Glazer, for starters. (Methodology: I'm counting anyone with one Jewish parent as a Jew. It was good enough for Hitler; it's good enough for me.) I'm sure there are tons more funny youthful Jews I haven't heard of because I am old and never leave my house.

I'm delighted that younger female comics don't seem to go as quickly for the Phyllis Diller/Joan Rivers–esque "I'm hideous" joke as their predecessors did, and they don't seem as quick to sneer at other women. I'd like to think that we're collectively teaching our daughters not to call other girls sluts and porkers, and that we're teaching our sons not to identify with frat-boy idiots.

## HOW HUMOR WILL HELP YOUR KID SUCCEED IN LIFE

As we've discussed, laughter is good for your health, helps build connections with others, and can help create identification with and sympathy for marginalized people. It can be a tool to talk about the world with your kid—its beauties and its terrors. Humor lets us identify with the little guy and laugh at jerks in power. It's a bonding opportunity: Reading silly books, telling jokes, and singing ridiculous show tunes together can make a disparate collection of individuals feel like a family unit. And yes, humor can be a way to identify with your heritage. Comedian Paul Reiser told the *Forward*, "When I hear my kids quote Mel Brooks records, it's as warm to me as if they quote the Torah."

Humor can also be a gift you offer your kid that will, when deployed correctly, help them advance at work. Studies have shown that people associate a sense of humor with intelligence and creativity, and indeed, that humor and creativity seem to be correlated. Robert Half International, an executive recruitment firm, surveyed 492 professionals and found that 91 percent believe humor is important for career advancement, while 84 percent think that people with a good sense of humor do a better job than those who aren't as funny. A 2012 study by the Bell Leadership Institute surveyed 2,700 employees in a variety of workplaces and found that a "sense of humor" and "work ethic" were considered by far the most important skills for strong senior managers—those two phrases were mentioned twice as often as any others. Jokes can briefly eliminate markers of status and make everyone feel part of a team. And a 2013 study in the *Leadership & Organization Development*

*Journal* found that employees perceived bosses who used self-deprecating humor to be kinder and more caring than bosses who weren't funny or who used negative humor.

How to help your kid develop skills that will be useful career-wise in the long run? Encourage them to poke mild fun at themselves rather than exploding at others or saying "I'm so stupid!" Encourage them to use humor that makes others feel good. (When Max was seven, she tucked into the spaghetti and meatballs I'd made, and when I asked how it was, she sighed and said, "You're an artist.") When a friend or family member is upset because they've messed up, urge your kid to make a gentle joke about how they've done something similar. (When Jonathan nearly smacked Josie while closing a car trunk, she shrugged, saying, "Heads are so last year.")

Academics who study workplace humor have found that strong leaders use humor to temper hard truths, to make people work hard and with enthusiasm for the task at hand, to avoid drama and stress in the office. Ineffective or bad boss humor reinforces status differences, creates distractions, or is simply a platform for the boss to waste people's time by showing off. (Basically, think about the boss on *The Office*—the American version or the British version, your call—and then DO NOT BE THAT.)

We want to raise kids who can laugh at themselves, who are able to joke in the *badkhan* tradition of poking fun at those in positions of authority rather than tearing down those who are already prone to getting ripped apart. We want to be the kind of parents who can giggle at the absurdity of raising children and laugh off most of the frustrations of toddler tantrums and adolescent eye-rolling.

There's an old Yiddish folktale (available in several

children's book versions—the one written and illustrated by Margot Zemach won a Caldecott Honor from the American Library Association) with the tagline, "It could always be worse." A poor family is crowded into a one-room hut and on the verge of killing each other, so they ask the rabbi what to do. The rabbi ponders, then tells them to bring their chickens, rooster, and geese into the house too. The family does, and lo and behold, the house is even more crowded! The family keeps going back to the rabbi for more help, and he keeps telling them to move in more livestock. Finally, he tells the family to move all the animals out of the house. And hey, everything is amazing and (relatively) quiet and peaceful. It's a miracle! The moral, of course, is that it could always be worse. This is worth remembering.

You want to raise a kid who isn't a drama queen (or king) and who can pivot and regroup when life gets challenging. And you want to be the kind of parent who appreciates the messy, chaotic, metaphorical-livestock-filled in-the-moment-ness of parenting. If you're doing it right, raising kids shouldn't be all joy and no fun.

## ∞ Mamaleh Methodology

1. **Don't be mean.** Don't use humor as a passive-aggressive (or hey, aggressive-aggressive) way to belittle your kid. Make sure your kid knows the difference between the kind of humor that embraces others and the kind that pushes them away.

2. **Don't take anything too seriously.** Kids go through phases and then pop out the other side. When I was in the thick of toilet training and sleep training and teething and breastfeed-

ing hell and mastitis and separation anxiety, the worry seemed all-encompassing. It ate my life. But now it's hard to remember the intensity of the emotions I felt then. The moral: Laugh whenever you can. Do not lose your cool. Or try not to lose it too often. This too shall pass.

3. **When someone tells a hateful joke, call them on it.** Teach your kid to do the same. There's no one answer about precisely how to respond: A "really, dude?" might be enough. An explanation of why the joke was offensive might help someone who is legitimately clueless. Other possible responses: "You're better than that." "I must have misunderstood you." "I know you're a kind person, so you may not realize what you just said. That joke makes you seem unkind." "What do you mean?" Or sometimes simply a raised eyebrow and a long pause can say it all.

*Chapter 9*

# Value Money
# (but Not Too Much)

With money in your pocket, you are wise, and you are handsome, and you sing well, too.

*—Yiddish proverb*

I have to admit something: Money freaks me out. I grew up middle class, with an educator mom and a psychiatrist dad who was more interested in public health and serving the truly mentally ill (he started a community mental health center and worked on a mobile medical van) than in making money. My parents conveyed that talking about money was tacky—we're from New England, after all—and that craving money was worse. I married a research and technology genius and serial entrepreneur whose income has varied widely; I'm a writer (magazines, TV, ghostwriting) who has occasionally made a six-figure income and usually made much less.

I don't like to talk about money and I don't like to think about money.

Which means I haven't always been the best exemplar for my kids, what with my own anxieties and ambivalence. I've sometimes been willfully clueless: When I was a freshman in college, my dad mocked me relentlessly when he saw my checkbook, in which I'd written "Stuff?" on an entry line. "STUFF!" he'd exclaim. "She bought STUFF!"

But part of being a good parent is conveying nuanced messages about money. The fact that I worry that we live beyond our means, that I worry about paying for college, that I worry about my husband's resentment about being the one with the steady gig and the health insurance . . . all these issues are worth talking to my kids about now that they're eleven and fourteen and old enough to understand complexity. I've learned that it's okay to talk to kids about subjects that make us uncomfortable, and *say* they make us uncomfortable. It's okay to let kids see our struggles.

I don't think I'm alone in my discomfort. Even though Jews tend to be excellent talkers, we seem to have a block about this one subject. Maybe once upon a time we were good at money talk, back when we were scrappy little immigrant families in which everyone pitched in to support the household and a big treat was a half-penny's-worth of chocolate babies. Today, we've got tougher choices to make: Now that we have achieved a level of comfort and status in society, and have actual meaningful income, how much do we give our kids? What do we expect from them in exchange, if anything? How important is keeping up with the Janowitzes? Why does talking about money make us so uncomfortable?

One thing that's helped me is making talk about money inextricable from talk about *choices* and *charity*. Judaism's attitude toward money can be summed up by a quote from

Rabbi Hillel, an important and beloved first century BCE rabbi and woodcutter: "If I am not for myself, who will be for me? And if I am only for myself, what am I?" In other words, taking care of your own is important . . . but so is looking out for others. I take this to mean you should be self-protective and support your family while always remembering that you're part of a larger community. If you're not a caring, kind, charitable person who supports the wider world, who are you, really?

Keeping Rabbi Hillel's dictum in mind means constantly making choices. How much do we spend and how much do we save? How much of our income do we give to charity? How much luxury do we need; what jobs do we pursue; where do we live that's both within our means and a source of like-minded community? In the past, money lending, selling, and trading were some of the few businesses open to Jews in many countries; when you're being booted every generation or so, you quickly learn that you better be able to take it with you. Money can't buy security, but it sure helps. So how do we teach kids to appreciate the value of a dollar, but to avoid becoming a greedy, corrupt schmuck?

## A HISTORY OF JEWS AND MONEY

Jews have always fretted about needing, getting, having too little, and wanting too much. The Torah and Talmud are full of exhortations about being ethical in business, starting with the Ten Commandments: "You shall not covet your neighbor's wife, or slaves, or ox, or ass, or anything that is your neighbor's." Our sage Maimonides theorized that "coveting" means wanting something so much you'll do pretty much anything to get it, including steal it. He said that when you covet, you put pressure on the other person to give the object of desire to you—and even if you pay him well for it, you're violating the commandment. Maimonides is pretty clear that the sin isn't actually about *feeling;* it's about *behavior.* (Not every commentator on the Torah agrees. Two Jews, three synagogues.) My takeaway: It's okay to admit that you want riches and comforts. You just can't act unethically to get them.

The Torah is also clear that craving money above all else leads nowhere good. The book of Ecclesiastes—*Kohelet* in Hebrew—when not providing song lyrics for the Byrds ("a time to love and a time to hate, a time for war and a time for peace") says pointedly that "a lover of money never has his fill of money, and a lover of wealth never has his fill of income." And Jewish legend offers a reason for the destruction of the Second Temple: People had begun to love money more than they loved each other.

The anti-Semitic stereotype is that Jews crave only money. But Jews have long thrived as researchers, humanitarians, and creative types. Jewish values—curiosity, education, literacy, a love of storytelling and debate and argument, suspicion of authority, dismay about the status quo and devotion to healing the world—have pushed us into fields that may or may not fill our pockets, but have satisfied our souls. Today, our position in majority culture has changed, which means that we (like all middle- and upper-class Americans) need to work to ensure that our children do not become entitled, money-grubbing little weenies.

There's a famous tale in *Pirkei Avot* in which a non-Jew snarkily approaches the rabbis Hillel and Shammai and says, "I want to convert to your religion, but only if you can teach me the whole Torah while I stand on one foot." Shammai chased him away with a hammer. (He was a builder as well as a rabbi.) Hillel responded differently. He said, "What is hateful to you, do not do to your neighbor. That's the whole Torah; the rest is commentary. Go and learn." What, then, does this variant of the Golden Rule mean, practically speaking? Basically, it means considering how you wouldn't want to be cheated; you wouldn't want to have someone lusting after your house or donkey; you wouldn't want to be disrespected. Of course, that's not everything there is to know about Judaism—the commentary is vital, as we've discussed, and that's why Hillel adds, "go and learn." You can't really learn the whole Torah standing on one foot. But not being a douche about money is a good start. The *Mekhilta,* an explication of the book of Exodus, says, "Whoever conducts his business dealings honestly is liked by humankind, and it is considered as though he has observed the entire Torah." (Ooh, shortcut!)

Judaism bans the worship of idols. And money can be an idol. Blind lusting after it distracts you from what's good and real, disconnects you from your community, makes you lose your sense of self. Again, from *Pirkei Avot:* "Who is rich? One who is content with one's portion." Rather than the pursuit of material wealth, our tradition stresses three things: *Torah, avodah,* and *gemilut hasadim.* Learning Torah, working hard, and doing good deeds for others. Sounds sappy, but really, is it such a bad way to live?

And you know what? You don't even have to go all-in on the Torah part. Let it stand in for learning, for self-improvement, for the commitment to keep one's focus on morality and our human obligation to one another. Jews have never believed that everyone has to be *Jewish* to be his or her best self, either. "The righteous of the nations of the world have a portion in the world-to-come," says *Tosefta Sanhedrin,* an ancient compilation of Jewish oral law. So there.

One thing Jews have always encouraged other Jews to spend money on is ritual. In the times and places where the Jewish community was well-off—Tunisia in the first century, thirteenth-century Barcelona, sixteenth-century Cairo, seventeenth-century Fez and Alexandria, early-twentieth-century Berlin and Turkey—synagogues were beautiful and elegant, and Jewish scrolls and books were gorgeously crafted. In the sixteenth through nineteenth centuries, Jews did a brisk business in *tkhines* (a Yiddishized version of the Hebrew word *tkhinot,* meaning supplications), prayer books specifically for women. They were written in Yiddish, the language of common speech, rather than Hebrew, the elevated language of traditional prayer. Many were written by women. They contained prayers for daily life: pregnancy and childbirth, infertility, recovering from illness, confessing sins, coping with widowhood . . . and making a good living.

(One thing that tickles me about *tkhines* is the way they were advertised—what translator Devra Kay calls the "unashamed, unsubtle combination of commercialism and piety." Then, as now, spirituality was a marketable commodity: If you have money (and even if you don't), you need feel no guilt about spending money on books and tools of self-betterment! A translation of the Torah into Yiddish, marketed to women, urged: "All you girls should not hesitate to sell your own dress or all your things to obtain the money with which to buy this.")

I don't think it's bad to market your products and sell

what you've got to the best of your ability. Just don't cheat anyone, and remember that the spirituality part of the equation actually *is* important.

The marketing of women's prayer books to women is an indication that despite all kinds of strictures placed on them in terms of how they could earn money, Jews have been good at figuring out where there was a market for a good or service and how to reach that market. When Jews were actually allowed to compete in business on a level playing field—such as in the late nineteenth century in parts of Western Europe and Russia—non-Jews were irked by how *good* Jews were at making money. Mark Twain observed, "I am persuaded that in Russia, Austria, and Germany nine-tenths of the hostility to the Jew comes from the average Christian's inability to compete successfully with the average Jew in business—in either straight business or the questionable sort. In Berlin, a few years ago, I read a speech which frankly urged the expulsion of the Jews from Germany; and the agitator's reason was as frank as his proposition. It was this: that eighty-five percent of the successful lawyers of Berlin were Jews, and that about the same percentage of the great and lucrative businesses of all sorts in Germany were in the hands of the Jewish race! Isn't it an amazing confession? It was but another way of saying that in a population of 48,000,000, of whom only 500,000 were registered as Jews, eighty-five percent of the brains and honesty of the whole was lodged in the Jews." Aw, shucks, Mr. Clemens.

Today, American Jews tend to be wealthier than the average citizen. A quarter of us have a household income of more than $150,000, compared to 8 percent of the rest of the country. And since we wait longer than average to have kids (one survey found that 52 percent of Jewish women between the ages of thirty and thirty-four are kid-free, compared with 27 percent of all American women that age), by the time they arrive we have more to spend on them. We also may be eager to buy them *stuff* as a way to sop our guilt at being working mothers—a recent Gallup poll found that 75 percent of college-educated women with kids under eighteen work outside the home, compared with only 48 percent of moms without a college degree . . . and the 2013 Pew Research Center's Portrait of Jewish Americans indicated that most of us are college graduates, and 28 percent of us have postgraduate degrees. What all this adds up to: We have to think harder about what having money means.

It's understandable to want our kids to be happy and have material rewards. But we're getting out of control. A 2011 study found that parents in households that bring in more than $102,000 spend more than twice as much on their children's enrichment (in terms of books, music lessons, computers, travel) as parents who earn around $62,000. Wealthier families spend not just *more* money, but a greater *percentage* of their money, on enrichment for kids—because they can. And a 2013 study found that the gulf in spending between the highest- and lowest-earning segments of America widened in the last two decades—poorer parents now spend less on their kids than they did in the past, probably because poorer today means really, *really* poorer.

On the one hand: Yay for spending money to make your children's lives more beautiful and elevated. But on the other: Uh, what about other people's kids?

It's smart to take a look back at the way Jews have historically paired having money with giving money away. Whether you're Jewish or not, whether you have a lot of disposable income or hardly any, you and your offspring can benefit from Jews' perspective on doing well and doing good.

## THE JEWISH HISTORY OF PAIRING MONEY WITH RIGHTEOUSNESS

The Hebrew word *tzedakah* is usually translated as "charity." But that's not what it actually means. What it really means is "righteousness." Giving charity, for us, is mandatory, part of being a good human. There is no talk of making money without talk of charity. It's incumbent upon us to make sure our children are aware that others have less than we do, to urge nonselfishness and generosity, to model the behavior we want to see, and to communicate the value of a dollar.

Let me call back Mark Twain, who observed that being Jewish was inextricably tied to charity. He noted that Jews took care of their own. For people who were frequently called parasites, they sure displayed nonparasitic behavior. "When [a Jew] is well enough, he works," Twain wrote. "When he is incapacitated, his own people take care of him. And not in a poor and stingy way, but with a fine and large benevolence. His race is entitled to be called the most benevolent of all the races of men. A Jewish beggar is not impossible, perhaps; such a thing may exist, but there are few men that can say they have seen that spectacle. The Jew has been staged in many uncomplimentary forms, but, so far as I know, no dramatist has done him the injustice to stage him as a beggar. Whenever a Jew has real need to beg, his people save him from the necessity of doing it. The charitable institutions of the Jews are supported by Jewish money, and amply. The Jews make no noise about it; it is done quietly; they do not nag and pester and harass us for contributions; they give us peace, and set us an example—an example which we have not found ourselves able to follow; for by nature we are not free givers, and have to be patiently and persistently hunted down in the interest of the unfortunate."

The man was correct. By the time Jews arrived in America, even pre–Civil War, they'd already replicated the social service institutions they'd established in the other countries around the world they'd lived in. Almost every Jewish community had a Hebrew Benevolent Society, and by the 1850s, cities with larger Jewish communities had the beginnings of Jewish federations, which provided help with family and children's services, caregiving, vocational assistance, health care, education, aging, disability aid, and burial societies. By the early 1900s, these federations were widespread. Both before and after the two world wars, they worked hard to raise funds for European Jewish communities. They still exist across the country today.

Nowadays Jews tend to be more economically comfortable than they often were in the past. But we're still very concerned with *tzedakah,* with righteousness. We're more integrated into the fabric of the wider culture than we once were, so our view of righteousness has expanded exponentially. We aren't just concerned about Jews' welfare; we worry about everyone's. We tend to vote for social services and assistance that benefit those less advantaged than we are, even when doing so directly and negatively affects our own pocketbooks.

The right-leaning sociographer Milton Himmelfarb had an aphorism: "Jews earn money like Episcopalians and vote like Puerto Ricans." Hmm. But yep, from midcentury onward, Jews tended to be wealthier than the average American but also more liberal. (Maybe that's why stereotypes of Jews are so contradictory: We're leftists, but we're capitalists! We're Marxists, but we're money-grubbers! Joseph Telushkin has noted research showing that the same non-Jews who believe the statement "Jews are always trying to push in where they are not wanted" *also* tend to believe the statement "Jews are clannish, always sticking together." Weird! But then again, maybe there's no conflict. Maybe we're planning to take over the world's money markets together, like a big Hanukah party held simultaneously at all the world's stock exchanges. But I doubt it.)

Himmelfarb was right: Jews identify with the Democratic Party by a ratio of three to one; only 22 percent of us identify with the Republican Party. (Except among the Orthodox, where 57 percent say they lean Republican and only 36 percent tilt toward Blue State sentiment.) I think this is tied to our views on money. Jews have historically cared about the downtrodden of all backgrounds, and today most Jews (according to Pew) think other groups are more oppressed than we are. Orthodox Jews may be closer to the rest of the American Right in considering themselves "values voters," concerned with the primacy of the "traditional family," and they may consider the Republican Party more sympathetic toward Israel. But younger non-Orthodox Jews tend to lean left on Israel and are unlikely to count Israel as one of their major issues when they go to the polls.

Our general belief that spreading righteousness is essential is reflected in our mania for "Mitzvah Projects," a trend in Bar and Bat Mitzvahs in which a kid does some kind of mandatory charitable donating and/or volunteering.

I am not nuts about Mitzvah Projects. I find them inauthentic. They're a hoop to jump through, along with learning a Torah portion and writing thank-you notes for iTunes gift cards. Just as the purpose of a Bar or Bat Mitzvah should be to prepare a child to become a participant in Jewish life with all its obligations, *tzedakah* should be integrated into the child's view of what it means to be a responsible grown-up.

In practice, most Mitzvah Projects seem to consist of asking your guests (who are already buying you the damn iTunes gift cards) to give to a random charity, singsonging about your deep dedication to this cause in your speech, and then forgetting about it a few weeks after you've put away all your today-I-am-a-man pens. Is this really productive? I already give *tzedakah* to the causes of my own choosing, and there are a zillion additional worthy causes I wish I could help. I feel bushwhacked when a kid *noodges* me to give to an organization they may or may not have researched extensively, that may or may not be well reviewed on sites like Charity Navigator and GuideStar, and that they may or may not really give two hoots about.

I'd rather see a kid use their own money and do thoughtful research on what kind of charity they want to support. My kids' Jewish camp has a tradition called MADIMOW, which stands for Making a Difference In My Own Way. Kids bring five one-dollar bills to camp, and while they're there, they research different causes and decide where to donate and how to allocate the money. Do you give it all to one organization? To five different ones?

I love this notion. We have a tzedakah box we put money in every week (uh, when we remember—another thing I need to do better) and we choose where to donate the money when it's full . . . but it wasn't until I read personal finance columnist Ron Lieber's *The Opposite of Spoiled: Raising Kids Who Are Grounded, Generous, and Smart About Money* that I realized we don't talk enough about where my husband and I donate *our* money. I asked the kids what causes they thought I supported. "Probably something Jewish?" Maxie said. I listed my charities (I'm of the give-a-little-to-a-lot-of-organizations school), which lean more toward women's health organizations than Jewish ones. (I do give to some Jewish ones, I promise.) We talked about why I liked each charity . . . and also about why I sometimes give money to homeless people and sometimes not. It's all about whim, and how close my wallet is, and how busy I am, and how instinctively I feel the need. Which is also why we need to give in an organized way in addition to following whims—whims are not focused or sustaining.

## TALKING TO KIDS ABOUT MONEY

It's vital for kids to understand that health, friendship, hard work, joy, creativity, and good works are more important than *things*. Study after study correlates materialism with anxiety and depression; studies on even very little children show that being generous makes kids happy. Giving to charity, spending on others, and thinking carefully about purchases can all mitigate the negative effects of growing up affluent, as so many kids today do.

In many ways my family has been lucky. Josie and Maxie were among the wealthier kids in their public elementary school, where a significant number of families qualified for free lunch. At their Hebrew school and synagogue, they were on the lower end of the economic spectrum. It was healthy for them to belong to two such different communities, to see up close and personal that rich and poor are relative concepts.

Jews today tend to freak out about the costs and over-the-top-ness of Bar and Bat Mitzvahs, but treatment of a prayerful event as a fashion show is nothing new. The eighteenth-century Lithuanian scholar Elijah ben Shlomo Zalman, known as the Vilna Gaon (the wise man of Vilnius) wrote to his wife, "Do not take your daughter to the synagogue where she will see girls of her age dressed in finery of which she is deprived. This may produce envy and gossip." Welcome to my world, Vilna Gaon.

We were fortunate that the first friend's Bat Mitzvah Josie attended was a low-key affair at a tiny congregation in Massachusetts, after which the kids made sandwiches at a homeless shelter. The second was a huge blowout at a New Jersey country club. As a result, Josie quickly saw that there are many ways to celebrate. When it was time for her own Bat Mitzvah, she chose something in between those two events—brunch at shul and a small party at The Strand bookstore. She gave each friend a book. There was no band, no DJ, just good food and a bunch of kids lying on the floor in fancy outfits reading.

I tell you this not to brag about my hyperliterate child (who forgets to feed the cats every damn day and is constitutionally unable to load a dishwasher), but to make the point that there are ways to push back against the prevailing culture's materialism, whether you're Jewish or not. In *The Opposite of Spoiled,* Lieber mentions a project at Brandeis Hillel, a Jewish day school in San Francisco, where parents realized they were spending $13,000 a year on Bar and Bat Mitzvah gifts. Hello. So they proposed a change: They'd pool their money and give each kid a small check and create a fund with the rest for kids to give away to a charity of their choice. The kids met with nonprofit executives and decided how to allocate money and got to experience the joy of giving away a bigger sum than any of them could raise or earn on their own. (When they told the director of the local Boys and Girls Club that they were giving her $3,000, she burst into tears.) The school wound up working the project into the seventh-grade curriculum, talking about charity as a value, the systemic causes of poverty, the role of local and national governments, and more. They explored making food budgets, bought groceries, and donated the food to a local food bank. Today, other schools have copied the curriculum.

Many generations of Jews have succeeded despite being poor, because we still had education and a tradition of literacy. Today's low-income kids aren't so blessed. Poor kids have rates of achievement as much as four years behind wealthy kids, and now even middle-class kids are falling behind too. Rich kids increasingly take up a disproportionate number of slots at competitive colleges. And inequities start early: A 2011 study by sociologist Sean F. Reardon, Professor of Poverty and Inequality in Education at Stanford, shows the gap in test scores between kids whose families are in the bottom 10 percent of income and kids whose families are in the top 10 percent; it has expanded by 40 percent. Nowadays, income is the single greatest predictor for how well kids will do in school. The upshot: The opportunities that once helped Jews just aren't there for today's poor families. It's incumbent on those of us who have benefited from America's blessings to give a leg up to those who haven't been so blessed.

## COPING WITH KIDS' MATERIALISM

My dad had an expression: "Don't be a *chazzer*!" That's Yiddish for "pig." (It's Hebrew, too, but my dad pronounced it the Yiddish way, for comic effect, to sound like an elderly Jew even when he was in his thirties.) Being a *chazzer* referred to everything from monetary greed to taking more than your share of the cookies to looking for a better parking place when there's a perfectly acceptable spot that's a ninety-second rather than fifteen-second walk to the Ocean State Job Lot entrance.

"Don't be a *chazzer*" is not a bad philosophy for living. Think about why you want something, and ponder why you want it so much. Do you (and your kids) understand the difference between wants and needs? You *need* pants. You *want* fancy jeans with artfully placed rips and embroidery on the back pockets that subtly telegraphs something to someone who is not you since you cannot, in fact, see your own ass when you are wearing the pants. (Unless you look over your own shoulder in mirrors a lot, like a low-wattage reality TV star.)

After talking to the wise personal finance writer Beth Kobliner, author of *Make Your Kid a Money Genius*, I told Josie that I would buy her new pants when she started looking like a highwater-sporting extra in a *Revenge of the Nerds* remake, but I would buy them only at Old Navy, Forever 21, or Uniqlo, where pants do not cost an arm and a leg. She loves vintage clothing, as do I, and we sometimes go thrifting for fun, but she knows if she wants something she does not need, she has to pay for it from her allowance.

Here is a fun fact: The Hebrew word for "item of clothing," *beged*, has the same root as the word for "betrayal." (We say "we have betrayed"—*bagadnu*—every year during the High Holidays liturgy, when we ritually beat our breasts during the *Ashamnu* prayer. This prayer is essentially Jewish confession, but without a priest to tell how many Hail Marys and Our Fathers we need to absolve us—which means we instead have to stew in our own anxiety, apologizing to everyone we've wronged, hoping God doesn't strike us down where we stand. Which could happen.)

The reason clothing is tied to betrayal: From the Garden of Eden on, clothing has been a source of anxiety and the locus of worries about deception and wiliness. The very first time the Torah mentions clothing, it's tied to Adam and Eve's betrayal of God's trust, shame in being naked, and desire to run away from consequences. Clothing is intricately connected to the first lie, the first punishment, and banishment from paradise. *Look at the betrayal your designer jeans represent, youth of today!*

Seriously, though, when you're young, you may well believe that if you have the right clothes, hair accessories, shoes, and jackets, you will be popular and happy. Our culture tells us it's so. One hopes that as an adult one outgrows this, but the profits of those who make designer merchandise indicate that many people haven't. Hectoring children for having crappy values or believing that expensive sneakers lead to happiness isn't helpful. What messages are they getting from you? From their school community? From mass media? Can you gently have a conversation about why you believe in spending money the way you do, and can you be authentic about your own desires? I think it's helpful as a parent to talk about the stuff you really wish you could have—a specific pair of designer shoes, a fancy-pants vacation in Morocco, a piece of original art by a favorite illustrator—and explain that even you, the all-powerful grown-up, cannot have everything your heart yearns for.

When it comes to spending money, again, pick the hill you want to die on. When you give your kid an allowance, you don't then get to carp and kvetch and *drei* and grumble when your kid just wants to buy endless Squinkies or Ninjago or Bionicles or Shopkins or Beanie Boos or whatever the hell the kids are into by the time you read this. I've read books and articles by experts who believe in giving kids an allowance tied to chores and experts who believe the opposite. Honestly, I'm agnostic. All I know is that giving to charity needs to be part and parcel of having spending money.

## LETTING KIDS MAKE MONEY DECISIONS

Having to prioritize is an important skill in adult life. We can't have all the things we want, and it's good for kids to learn that when they're young.

My kids know that when I wrote for TV I had a pretty high and steady salary, but I worked until late at night and cried a lot. They know that when I worked for print magazines, back when there were these things called print magazines, I achieved a degree of success in which people actually paid me *not* to write for other magazines. But now there are many fewer magazines, and they hire writers much younger than I, and they assign much shorter stories than the kind I used to write. I make way less money than I once did. My kids know this too.

Jonathan and I have talked to Josie and Maxie about

what kinds of trade-offs we might employ to make our financial lives less stressful, and what their own goals might be in terms of the lives they want to lead when they grow up. We've asked them to ponder their own money values. Would they prefer to have exciting but unsteady employment, or to have money socked away for the future even if their day-to-day life is drearier than they'd like, or to live somewhere exciting but expensive or less safe but more lively or more boring but affordable? Would they prefer to live in the city, suburbs, or country . . . and what kinds of jobs might they do to support themselves in all these different places? When the kids talk about wanting to be actors or writers, I ask how they'll earn a living while struggling for their break. What kinds of sacrifices will you make if you commit to chasing your dream?

Delayed gratification for a worthy reward never hurt anybody. I think the exercise of imagining working hard to achieve a glamorous goal is a perfectly fine one. And in the here and now, you can encourage your kid to save up for something he or she wants. Strategize about how they could earn money to get it. Even little kids can do extra things to earn money. (Jonathan has taught Maxie to scan business cards, use the paper shredder, and make cocktails at parties. She can mix up a fine gin and tonic, Moscow Mule, or Dark and Stormy. Come over sometime.)

Finally, I like the notion of telling kids that school is their job. We all have work to do, and alas, one's job isn't always replete with roses and rainbows. We do it anyway, because it is our *job*, and because fulfilling our commitments makes us feel good and makes us a *mensch*, a good person. But as kids get older, adding a job-job to the school-job can be a good idea. In *Make Your Kid a Money Genius*, Beth

Kobliner points out studies showing that college students who work in on-campus jobs for up to about twenty hours a week get higher grades than students who don't work at all. Why? One theory is that on-campus work makes these kids feel more engaged in and committed to their college community, which motivates them to work harder on all fronts. (The better-grades correlation didn't hold true for kids with off-campus jobs.) Beth also cites a national study by researchers at the University of California-Merced showing that kids who help pay for college feel more invested in their education, perhaps because, as she says, they have "skin in the game." And having a job may help kids structure their time better.

Ultimately, everything comes back to Rabbi Hillel's question: "If I am not for myself, who will be for me? And if I am only for myself, who am I?"

Being sure we're attuned to giving both financial help and kindness to those who need it is good for parents, kids, and the world in general. Settlement worker and activist Jane Addams (1860–1935) once said, "In the unceasing ebb and flow of justice and oppression we must all dig channels as best we may, that at the propitious moment somewhat of the swelling tide may be conducted to the barren places of life." Indeed, what more can any of us do?

## 𝟞𝟞 Mamaleh Methodology

1. Integrate charity and righteousness into your family's life. Talk to kids about supporting businesses that take good care of their employees or help out in the community— neighborhood farmers' markets, the card shop that sponsors

a Little League team, the *tchotchke* store that donates gift certificates to the PTA auction. On vacation, avoid buying crappy, unmemorable cookie-cutter souvenirs (probably made in China rather than the location you're visiting), and choose to spend money at the local ice cream parlor or carousel, the thrift store or the used record shop.

2. **Remember that kids notice everything.** Homeless people on the sidewalk. Your tossing of charity solicitations into the recycling bin unopened, accompanied by bitter muttering. The dismissive lie behind "Oh, honey, I can't buy you that because I don't have any cash." (They see your credit cards.) They'll note the gulf between what you say and what you do with your money.

3. **Explain advertising and marketing.** As kids get older, it's also good to show them the machinery of selling. We get all kinds of subtle and not-so-subtle messages—of all sorts about how we should spend our money, and it's part of your job as an educator to show them we don't make choices in a vacuum.

4. **Make it clear that using plastic is still spending money.** Make sure kids understand early on that those flat things in your wallet are money, not magic. Explain how credit works, and talk about living within your means.

## Chapter 10

# Cultivate Spirituality and Model *Tikkun Olam*

Let [children] be sure that every little deed counts, that every
word has power, and that we do, everyone, our share to redeem
the world, in spite of all absurdities, and all the frustrations,
and all the disappointment. And above all, remember that the
meaning of life is to live life as if it were a work of art.

—*Abraham Joshua Heschel*

Spirituality isn't easy. It's not easy for anyone, but it's ultra-
knotty for Jews. The word *Israel*—which was the name for
a people before it was the name for a country—means "one
who struggles with God." In the Torah, the story goes,
Jacob is preparing finally to face his brother, Esau, many
years after stealing his birthright. The evening before the
meeting, an angel comes and wrestles with Jacob. Jacob
wins and refuses to let go until the angel gives him a blessing. The angel does. And then he tells Jacob that his new
name is Israel, because he's wrestled with faith and stayed
standing. This story is an indication that struggling with
God is integral to the very notion of who we are as people.

The grappling is an integral part of the process. It's
visceral, integrally connected to others, sweaty and chal-

lenging. Spirituality should not be individualistic and narcissistic, not patchouli scented or good-vibes-y.

I'd argue that Judaism posits that spirituality shouldn't be a solo act, focused entirely on the self. Judaism ties spirituality to community and to action. "When two people relate to each other authentically and humanly, God is the electricity that surges between them," Martin Buber once said. True spirituality is not only about our relationship to the self or the divine, but also to each other. That essential sense of connection to other people is part of why so many Jews have become doctors, scientists, and social justice activists. Virtue is not in our DNA (as with intelligence, I don't believe Jews are born with any better raw material than other people); it's the values we've transmitted that have made us do so well collectively. I'd argue that it's why we've become successful artists, songwriters, performers; we have insight into the human condition because from childhood we've been brought up to consider the feelings of others.

## RELIGION VS. SPIRITUALITY

Religion should involve collective work and music and shared endeavor, and most of all, it should be a framework for social justice.

An essential concept in Judaism is *tikkun olam,* usually translated as "healing the world." It means acts of lovingkindness, and participation in the ongoing process of creation. The sixteenth-century mystic Isaac Luria told a story that to create the world, God needed to make room, to contract God's divine self. It's like the opposite of the Big Bang.

Just as parental pulling back helps our kids grow, God's pulling back made space for human agency and goodness. In this legend of creation, God poured all the divine light into vessels, but God's power was so great the vessels shattered, sending shards all over the world. Our job as humans, and as parents, is to complete the divine work of creation by gathering those shards of goodness. We repair the world.

*Tikkun olam* is not optional. "You are not obligated to complete the work, but neither are you free to desist from it," says *Pirkei Avot, Ethics of the Fathers*. We all have to do our share.

There's a reason I have little tolerance for people who enjoy smiling beatifically while saying "I'm a rilly rilly spiritual person?" It's not just that they are annoying. It's that religion is a team sport in which spirituality is just one play. The ultimate goal of belonging to a faith tradition is to connect to something greater than yourself—to do good, to learn and teach, to have rigor in your life. "Spirituality" in Western culture frequently is tied to a lot of talk about self-forgiveness. In *Eat Pray Love,* when our narrator is meditating on a roof and has a vision in which she suddenly knows her ex-husband forgives her, I wanted to smack her on her invisible wannabe culturally appropriative bindi. You don't get to *decide* you're forgiven. That's a gift someone else gets to grant. All you get to do is apologize. Think of other, not self.

Meditation *à la hippie* can be a beautiful way to help us focus and calm our minds, but it's not the end goal—at least, I hope it's not. "All real living is meeting," Martin Buber said. True spirituality doesn't take place in your head or in wishful dreamspace.

The two aspects of religion I connect with the most are

*tikkun olam* and singing. I have a mediocre voice, but lifting it in song is at the heart of my personal spiritual connection. I don't get to sing in a group very often, unless I'm belting out "Schadenfreude" from *Avenue Q* with my family in the car. I used to sing the girls to sleep, but they're old now. (Maxie still sometimes asks me to sing "Soft Kitty" from *The Big Bang Theory* at bedtime.) But as a Conservative Jew, I can feel at home in almost any Conservative or Reform synagogue, because I know the songs and feel connected—emotionally, harmonically, spiritually, and physically—to others when we all sing together. Even when I don't know the people I'm praying with, I'm part of their community—and they're part of mine—when we sing. The thing I miss most about going to Jewish summer camp is the singing.

For me, the God part is nearly incidental. (For other Jews, God is entirely absent, and that's fine. More on them in a bit.) I don't pray in the hope of getting an answer. I tend to think of God as a *Star-Wars*-esque Force that, unlike the Jedis' version, is impossible to bend to one's will. To think about God deliberately snubbing the prayers of people with critically ill children, or to say there is some greater purpose to suffering, seems terribly cruel to me. My mom always says, "God is not a butler." Whatever your conception of God, God is not an entity that is waiting around to do your bidding. When athletes say God helped them win a game, I always wonder why God forsook the other team.

Maybe God is some kind of free will that causes us to choose good, to listen to our *yetzer hatov*. Maybe God is the invisible, evolutionarily driven desire to be altruistic. Maybe it's a process set in place during the Big Bang that has a definite beginning and ending, with all kinds of possibilities in the middle. Honestly, I don't know and I don't really care. Sometimes I find it comforting to think that there's a greater force at play in our lives, but more often I find it maddening and most of the time I don't think about it at all. People far smarter than I have struggled with the notion of why pray when it's not at all clear that God is going to pitch in. Someone once asked Abraham Joshua Heschel, "If God is not going to interfere, if God is not going to intervene, if God is not going to help, then what is the role of prayer?" Heschel answered, "First of all, let us not misunderstand the nature of prayer . . . The primary purpose of prayer is not to make requests. The primary purpose of prayer is to praise, to sing, to chant. Because the essence of prayer is a song, and man cannot live without a song."

## HOW TO SPIRITUALIZE YOUR OFFSPRING

Jewish mothers have historically conveyed the values of *Torah, avodah,* and *gemilut chasadim* (as a reminder, that's "learning Torah, working hard, and doing good for others") to their kids, and they're still relevant today. I believe it's possible to stress these values while being an atheist, an agnostic, or even (gasp) a non-Jew. To me, "Torah" means being thoughtful about history and values, not just about textual study. I think you, the reader, can define Torah to mean the values of teaching and learning, of knowing your own history, of choosing illumination over ignorance.

As we've discussed, Judaism is a home-centric religion. Lighting Shabbat and Passover candles, keeping a kosher kitchen, making traditional holiday foods—these tend to be the province of the mother. Research shows that in America today, women tend to be more religious than men—in terms of commitment, involvement, and belief. Jewish women married to non-Jewish men are much more likely to raise children who identify as Jews than Jewish men married to non-Jewish women. A 2002 survey of Jewish college freshmen found that those with Jewish mothers were more than twice as likely to identify as Jews as those with Jewish fathers. In short, the woman is the one who will teach a child how to be religious, spiritual, or connected to a faith tradition.

Kids like to feel a connection to a faith tradition. (Even if they might be bored and squirm their way through a weekly religious service.) The most recent Pew study on America's Changing Religious Landscape found that 79 percent of kids said their religion was important to them. I think it makes them feel connected to something larger than themselves; it's a source of identity and comfort and community. And we, the parents, can help them get there, using songs, group volunteerism, worship with a collective of people who share our values, stories of our own family and religious history, as well as jokes and narratives that reflect our morals.

Ritual and mindfulness, too, can make kids feel spiritual. A recent study by researchers at Harvard and the University of Minnesota at Minneapolis found that watching someone perform a ritual—say, uncorking a bottle of wine—doesn't affect the pleasure of drinking it, but *being* the person who uncorks the wine does. Mixing a pitcher of lemonade made people enjoy drinking the lemonade more than people who'd merely watched the lemonade being made. Involve your kids in the rituals of family life: cooking, setting the table, checking your helmet, bike chain, wheels, and brakes before going for a family ride. Jonathan and Maxie are inveterate container gardeners; to them, gardening is a meditative, shared, visceral experience of connection with the earth. To me, it is approximately as fun as watching paint dry, only not quite as interesting. To each their own.

Watching our kids wonder at the world can fuel our own. When Josie was not quite four, I asked her if she remembered fireworks from the previous Independence Day. She literally gasped and said, "Yes! You go on the roof and watch and they go up and up, more and more, pop-pop-popping like bubbles and there are always more-more-more." It was unintentional poetry, and it had been a very long time since I'd thought about the miracle fireworks had once felt like to me. When Maxie was two, she saw whole and uncut grapes for the first time. (I'd been neurotic about cutting them in half until then, having had to perform the Heimlich maneuver on Josie midflight to Wisconsin—my dear daughter had stuffed an entire chocolate chip cookie into her mouth.) When Max opened Josie's lunchbox after school and saw the leftover Baggie of grapes in a cluster still attached to their stems, I watched a series of confused expressions pass over her face. Finally she said, "Gapes . . . balloons?" Her sense of discovery made me feel as though I were watching her see how the universe fit together. We need to take the time to appreciate these little moments in our parenting lives.

## RELIGIOUS PEOPLE ARE NOT ALL KNEE-JERK, SCIENCE-DENYING, ANTIPLURALISTIC, JUDGMENTAL JERKFACES

The stereotype of a person of faith is that of someone politically rightward-leaning and repressive. (One reason I love

Stephen Colbert is that as a devout Catholic who's also funny and tolerant, he razes this narrow-minded portrait.) The stereotype is false. A 2013 survey of 2,002 Americans by the Public Religion Research Institute in partnership with the Brookings Institution found that one in five Americans could be classified as religious progressives. I count myself among their number. We're people who feel connected to our faith traditions, but our theological and social outlook is liberal rather than conservative. Maybe one reason so few people know about us is that we don't tend to push God on others. The study found that only 29 percent of religious progressives think a person has to believe in God to lead a moral life, compared to 74 percent of religious conservatives.

In sheer numbers, there are more religious conservatives than progressives in America . . . but that may be changing. According to a 2013 study by the Public Religion Research Institute in partnership with the Brookings Institution, millennial religious progressives actually outnumber religious conservatives, and they're a far more diverse group. Religious progressives are also far more passionate than nonreligious liberals (and of course, far *far* more passionate than religious conservatives) about correcting income inequalities and helping the poor. That's *tikkun olam*.

I like the notion of folks joining forces with people of other faiths to work together for a better world. As far as I'm concerned, that's part of the spiritual direction I give my kids: Being a person of faith means being an advocate for others, whether they share your traditions or not.

## BRINGING *TIKKUN OLAM* INTO YOUR ACTUAL, PRACTICAL, REAL LIFE

Start 'em young, focusing on building awareness of others as opposed to self. When Josie was three, I started talking to her about kids who don't have toys. She had more than she could possibly play with. (Oldest grandchild, on both sides of the family.) We live literally across the street from a homeless shelter. I started talking up how important it was to share what we have, how her least favorite toys could make a child in the shelter feel happy.

Predictably, everything I pulled out of the toy bin suddenly became THE MOST IMPORTANT TOY EVER IN THE HISTORY OF TOYS. There was lying on the ground sobbing. I remained resolute. I had her make a separate pile of stuff we would NEVER, EVER GIVE AWAY, so she could see that I was not determined to turn her into a Dickens character. We cleaned the plastic toys with Windex and gave the soft toys a spin through the washer and dryer. Then we took them over to the shelter and knocked on the plexiglass door.

A nice older gentleman in thick glasses answered the door. Josie, who eventually perked up at the notion of being regarded as a noble little human being, stood by my side as I explained that she wanted to give the toys she was too old for to kids who were staying there. The man took them and thanked us, then said, "Just a minute!" He left us at the door and disappeared for a moment, then came back with a giant tub of Magic Markers. "Here's a gift for you, too!" he said.

Josie's eyes bugged. At home I did not allow her to use

markers, after an incident involving our living room wall becoming a Cy Twombly installation. I'd told her while grimly scrubbing with Magic Eraser that markers were a PRIVILEGE, not a RIGHT, and they were in TIME-OUT until she was old enough to be TRUSTED WITH THEM. Now, for the cost of a few stuffed animals she didn't even *like* anymore, this dude had given her the forbidden fruit, Eve's apple, the most alluring thing in the world in her tiny mind. I wanted to say to the guy, *Sir! You are ruining my lesson of sacrifice and acts of loving-kindness! We don't get fucking markers for* mitzvot*!* But I decided that everything happens for a reason, and I let her carry the markers home. "I hope you realize you're not getting markers every time we do a good deed," I muttered. She was oblivious. And she did eventually learn that good deeds are generally marker-free. Though a couple of years later, casting her eyes angelically upward, she informed me, "I would like to give my old toothbrush to the poor."

In her turn, Maxie made her first visit to the shelter, also at three. The same man answered the door. Maxie handed over a bag of outgrown clothing and boring toys. "We're doing a *mitzvah*! Helping other people is a *mitzvah*!" she told the guy. He looked confused, but smiled and said thank you. The door closed, and we headed back down the block. Suddenly the door swung back open. "*Shalom! Shalom!*" the man yelled excitedly after us. As you probably know, "shalom" is Hebrew for hello, good-bye, and peace. It was clear that he'd retrieved the memory of a word he'd learned long ago. It was a moment of connection between a Jewish toddler and a goyish old man, and it was awfully sweet.

You and your kid don't have to do astonishing, creative things to do *tikkun olam*. Small acts can be powerful. But it's important to do work that meets an existing need (as opposed to yay, *we wanna help hunger, let's collect cans of old beets!*). It's vital for upper-income kids not to see themselves as heroic rescuers of downtrodden peoples, ennobled by consorting with the rabble. Make sure your kids know about the vast numbers of people working in their own communities to make change. They're heroes, not victims. (As the midrash says, "More than the wealthy person does for the poor, the poor person does for the wealthy.") Making sure kids are educated by reading books about diverse communities and by learning about injustices throughout history (not just those perpetrated on the Jews) is as important as refraining from charging in with a savior complex and a lack of historicity thinking you're a champion.

## IT'S NOT ABOUT YOU

The twelfth-century philosopher and physician Maimonides created a metaphorical ladder of righteousness, with each rung higher up than the one before. The lowest rung is giving money with resentment. The highest is helping someone to become self-supporting. As Maimonides wrote, "It is with regard to this that Scripture says: 'Then thou shalt strengthen him: Yea, though he be a stranger or a sojourner: that he may live with thee' (Leviticus, 25:35). The meaning is: Strengthen him before he falls and needs to be supported by others." My takeaway from this is that keeping people from falling into poverty—and helping them climb out—is a true Jewish value. Even if they're a stranger to you. Even if they don't share your faith or background. The whole "pull yourself up by your bootstraps" thing is not our tradition. It's also willfully naive—especially in times when many people don't even have boots—and naïveté is not something Jews have historically had the luxury of possessing.

Showy stunts like the bucket challenges that periodically roar through social media aren't very Jewish. They create a performance opportunity, a way to put a spotlight on yourself for your virtue. They may not support the most needy—they support whoever was lucky enough to come up in your feed or with a viral gimmick. If you give to one organization (or even do an act that "raises awareness" without actually donating), you may feel "Okay, I've done enough." Psychologists use the term "moral licensing" for the phenomenon of feeling you've done something virtuous leading you to feel excused from doing other virtuous things. If you see yourself as good, you unconsciously give yourself permission to be bad, or let yourself off the hook about doing more good. I wonder how much "hashtag activism," shooting off tweets and posts on social media about the outrage of the moment, prevents more meaningful engagement. (You've tweeted! You've done your share!) Raising awareness of an issue is great, but beware of that constituting moral license to do nothing else. Given that we have finite resources in terms of both time and money, make sure you actually do the work in addition to sharing your outrage.

## MAKE *TIKKUN OLAM* INTO FAMILY TIME

Vexingly, it takes longer to involve kids in doing *mitzvot* than to do the damn things yourself. Kids haven't developed the muscles yet. You have to walk them through every step and explain the whys as you go. It's so tiring. But as Heschel put it, "We don't need more textbooks. We need textpeople." This is another way to say, "Embody the life you want others to lead."

It helps to make virtue into fun family time. Josie and I have a project we do together every year. Josie came to share my obsession with the Triangle Factory Fire, New York City's worst workplace disaster before 9/11. On March 25, 1911, a fire broke out on the factory's eighth floor; 146 workers, most of them young Jewish and Italian girls who'd been locked into the workroom so the bosses could be sure they weren't shirking or stealing, died. The fire department's tallest ladders only reached the sixth floor. Girls clung to the window ledges while the flames licked at them; some jumped in desperation, shattering the sidewalks. Can any New Yorker who lived here during 9/11 not visualize what that looked and sounded like?

My family lives in a tenement building not far from where the factory stood. Furthermore, my husband is distantly related to Max Steuer, the coldly brilliant, much-hated hotshot lawyer who defended the factory owners. (I did not learn this until after we'd named our younger daughter Maxie Steuer. Oops.)

Josie picked up a Triangle chapter book—an easy reader, not too terrifying, about a young Italian girl and a young Jewish girl who become friends in the factory and dramatically help each other escape the fire—and was instantly hooked. (I'd cleverly left it on a low shelf in her room and said nothing about it. If I'd said, "Read this," it would be gathering dust there still. Holla, Judy Blume.) A few weeks after she read it, I learned about a participatory art project called CHALK, created by an artist named Ruth

Sergel who lived on our block. Every year, shortly before the anniversary of the tragedy, Ruth e-mails a name and address of a Triangle fire victim to anyone who wants to participate. On the day itself, we all fan out across the city to write a victim's name in chalk in front of the building in which they lived. Beneath the name, we write the person's age, address, and "Died in the Triangle Fire, March 25, 1911." Sergel's website has a clickable map of all the victims' addresses—they're heavily clustered in the East Village and Lower East Side, where we live.

Every year since Josie was seven (she's fourteen as I write this), she's chalked with me. At first, when there were fewer participants, we chalked several names. Now that more New Yorkers know about Ruth's project, we only get one name: that of Kate Leone, at fourteen the youngest fire victim. Josie has felt a special bond with her and has written her name since the beginning. Kate's loss is visceral to her. She says, "I keep getting older and Kate is always the same age. This year I'll actually be older than she ever got to be." CHALKers write names in front of tenements that look much as they did a hundred years earlier and in front of modern glass buildings and in front of empty lots. The experience of chalking is so immediate—crouching or sprawling on the ground while people stare at you, feeling conspicuous, trying to print neatly, thinking about where to tape the informational flyer. When you chalk in front of an address that no longer exists, or a building that's become a giant gentrified monstrosity, it's instructive to reflect on whatever's taken the tenement's place. One year we chalked for Rosie Brenman and her sister Surka. (According to David Von Drehle's book *Triangle: The Fire That Changed America,* their brother Joseph also worked at the Triangle and survived the blaze.) Another victim, eighteen-year-old Fannie Hollander, lived at the same address. Did they all walk to work together? Maybe Fannie had a crush on Joseph. Maybe the Brenman sisters giggled together quietly about Fannie's hairdo. The project makes us ponder people's lives, not just their deaths.

CHALK is an act of *tikkun olam* in that it's an act of honor and remembrance, a reminder that we need to continue protecting the most vulnerable and that sweatshops still exist. We've met other adult-and-kid CHALKers and walked with them; we've chatted with people whose stoops we were writing on. One year we met a local graffiti artist named Angel Ortiz, who'd worked with Keith Haring as a teenager. As Josie chalked Kate's name, Ortiz drew radiant babies and squiggles all around it.

CHALK is also a way for Josie and me to discuss the labor movement, an entire galaxy of *tikkun olam*. Jewish women had heroic roles in this movement, trying to make lives better for poor workers of all backgrounds. Rose Schneiderman (the cofounder of the ACLU who coined the phrase "Bread and Roses," as in "the worker must have bread, but she must have roses too"), Clara Lemlich (subject of the aforementioned lovely children's picture book *Brave Clara,* a tiny woman who led the shirtwaist strike in New York City), Belle Moskowitz (who advised NYC governor Al Smith on public health, poverty, and education), and many more Jewish women fought tirelessly to end child labor, make safer workplaces and saner hours, and ensure fair pay and workers' rights. Later, of course, Jewish women became leaders of the feminist movement: Emma Goldman, Annie Nathan Meyer, Maud Nathan, Betty Friedan, Bella Abzug,

Shulamith Firestone, Susan Brownmiller, Susan Faludi, Gloria Steinem, Letty Cottin Pogrebin, and many more. These women worked for pay equity and women's rights to safety, autonomy, and control of their own bodies.

"To think of others is as natural to the Jewish woman as to breathe," Belle Moskowitz said in 1917. You needn't be Jewish to think about exemplars of the behavior you want to see in your kids, by sharing stories and books and talking about virtuous acts you see in your community and in the world.

## HEALING THE SCHOOL: BULLIES, BYSTANDERS, AND BUTTINSKIES

Jews have no monopoly on social justice. All of us have an obligation to ensure that our kids care about the lives of people who are not necessarily like us. As Heschel said, "God did not make a world with just one color flower. We are all made in God's image."

One *tikkun olam* lesson we should all be teaching our children is to stand up when someone else is being bullied. Studies indicate that bullying often takes place in front of an audience (as many as nine in ten cases), but kids who witness bullying defend the victim less than 20 percent of the time. University of Illinois psychologist Dorothy Espelage found that sixth- and seventh-grade boys who didn't bully but who were friends with bullies were less willing to intervene when they saw bullying in action. If you have a kid who is considered "cool" (I have not been so blessed, since my husband and I are geeks who have raised geeks),

213

your kid has social capital. They can use it for the forces of good! But if your kid's school isn't encouraging these small acts of kindness, it's up to you to encourage them.

As a parent, you can make sure the language you use at home is slur-free, and you can talk about why tolerance and acceptance of differences are vital qualities. As Emily Bazelon points out in her terrific book *Sticks and Stones: Defeating the Culture of Bullying and Rediscovering the Power of Character and Empathy,* study after study shows that the best way to prevent the harassment of gay students is to make it unacceptable. Saying that you love the sinner but hate the sin does not fly. Schools and camps need to convey that slurs and taunts are immoral, and parents can and should talk to principals to be sure the message is getting through.

My own tenth-grade English teacher used to prance in front of the classroom with a limp wrist extended, making fun of "little Wally Whitman, shrieking his poems to the ocean." Ugh. Teachers, coaches, and counselors still fail to curtail the use of hate speech, and parents have an important role to play in making sure the world is a safe space for all. My kids have gay uncles, so we're a step ahead of the game here, but I still wasn't sure how Maxie would react when she was four, and we were visiting San Francisco and drove through the Castro, the historic gay neighborhood. As we stopped at a light, a fabulously dressed drag queen crossed in front of the car. Maxie stared, and I worried. But then Maxie yelled out the window, "I LOVE YOU, COLORFUL LADY!" (Let me assure you I am no perfect exemplar. I'm still struggling to banish the word *retard* from my vocabulary. I grew up with it, and when I'm tired or careless, it slips out. It's awful and wrong, and I've made sure my kids know I'm ashamed.)

*Tikkun olam* should be a big tent. Jews have no monopoly on persecution and trauma, even though some of us want to play the Holocaust as a tribulation trump card. Six! Million! Ovens! Beat *that*, other marginalized groups! Yeah, no. Life is not a suffering competition. It's our job to ensure that as our kids grow, they work to end ongoing, systemic inequities in their own cultural groups and in the wider world.

The book of Deuteronomy commands, *"Tzedek, tzedek tirdof"*—Righteousness, righteousness should you pursue. We need to right wrongs, support the underdog, and fix what's broken, even when it's hard and uncomfortable work. A lot of people who become active in doing social justice as adults can't really articulate why: "It's just the right thing to do," they say. It's what a lot of Christian rescuers said after the Holocaust, when asked why they risked their own lives to help Jews. But one study of helpers and bystanders during the Holocaust found that the majority of Christian rescuers had something in common: They came from loving homes. *Middot* (the Hebrew word for "virtues") are, in my mom's words, "caught, not taught." When you grow up in an atmosphere of kindness, you're more willing to imperil yourself to help others—even people you don't know. This is my ultimate goal in raising my daughters: raising empathetic humans. (Chris Rock said that one's ultimate goal is to keep one's daughters off the stripper pole. Which, I grant you, is also valid.)

## PRAYER, MEDITATION, AND REFLECTION

There's a nineteenth-century Hasidic story about an illiterate peasant boy who came to synagogue with his father on Rosh Hashanah. The little boy had no idea how to pray. When he and his father arrived, he watched with wide eyes as everyone else swayed and murmured and clutched their books. He asked his father, "What should I do?" His father muttered, "Just be quiet and listen to the prayers. That's enough." But the boy wanted to participate. His father hissed, "Shh! You don't know these prayers!" The boy thought for a moment, then said, "I'm going to whistle to God the way I whistle to my flock of sheep." And so he did. The father was mortified and enraged, but the boy whistled with focus and bliss. The story has it that the boy's heartfelt whistle made all the gates of heaven burst open, causing the prayers of the entire congregation to be heard.

There is no one right way to pray. (If your house of worship implies that there is, you're going to the wrong house of worship.) Whatever your faith tradition, there are only two things I think you need: *ruach* and *kavannah*. *Ruach* is a joyful, inviting spirit (it literally means "breath"), the kind of engagement you feel when you cheer for a beloved sports team. *Kavannah* is focused intent and inner devotion. They bring bliss, peace, absorption.

The embodiment of *kavannah* is Hannah in the Bible. She goes to the sanctuary at Shiloh to pray for a child. She's desperate, moving her lips silently, tears running down her face. She tells God that if God will only give her a son, she will give her son to the priesthood as soon as he's been weaned. The high priest, Eli, takes one look at this lady and thinks she's drunk; he tries to kick her out. She explains that she's sober; she's just pouring out her heart to God. Eli realizes he's been a schmuck and blesses her. God answers her prayer, and she becomes the mother of the prophet and judge Samuel, whose name means "God heard me."

I find these stories sweet and moving even though I don't believe in a God who intercedes personally in prayer. I like that these tales and prayers are old, a tie to the past. I think children, too, can understand that stories are powerful even if they're just stories.

## SPIRITUALITY IS A LEARNING PROCESS

No one is born knowing how to behave in a restaurant. You learn how to behave in a restaurant by going to a restaurant. So as parents, we take children (early in the evening, before crowds and toddler meltdowns) to restaurants (not hipster and/or schmancy restaurants) and we prepare them (by telling them how we behave, and by providing distractions like Cheerios and crayons) for a life of eating (God willing) in restaurants. We hope that if we do a good job, our child will not become an adult who undertips, snaps at serving staff, shrieks with deafening laughter, jabbers on their phone throughout the meal, or takes duckface selfies.

This slow process of immersive education is how you approach going to synagogue or church. Take your kid to children's services that are designed to be accessible, short, fun, and loud. As kids get older, make dates to go with their friends and their friends' parents. Pair services with a nice family walk or brunch.

In *Derekh Chayyim* (*The Way of Life,* a moral poem),

Menahem de Lonzano, who lived in Jerusalem in the early part of the seventeenth century, wrote, "Nowadays there are children who come to synagogue to provide punishment to those who bring them. They come to profane the sanctity of the house of our God, to play there as if they were out in the street. They make merry, they beat each other up, this one laughs and that one cries, this one talks and that one shouts, they run hither and yon. Some of them even urinate in the synagogue . . . Sometimes one of the parents gives a child a book, which the child throws on the ground or tears into a dozen pieces. The end of the matter is that because of their stupid noise, the worshippers lose all concentration, and the heavenly name is profaned. The one who brings children like this to synagogue, far from being worthy of reward, ought to be worried about retribution . . . The children will grow up with bad behavior and weird qualities." *Weird qualities.*

No one wants peeing, but most of us do want a looser atmosphere of worship. I left the first synagogue we joined, when Josie was a baby, because I sat behind an old lady at a Friday night *Kabbalat Shabbat* (welcoming the Sabbath) service who gave me the fisheye every time Josie cooed. Then we went to a family service that felt like a private club; no one even said hi to us. We switched to another synagogue that felt more welcoming.

Today, both my kids are comfortable in the synagogue. They go to children's services, attend friends' Bar and Bat Mitzvahs, have "pizza in the hut" (dinner in the synagogue's *sukkah* in the fall), stuff their faces at the ice cream party on *Shavuot* (harvest festival when dairy foods are a tradition), and perform in Hebrew school plays and in the Purim *shpiel* (goofy play that tells the Purim story). Now that Josie has become a Bat Mitzvah, she reads Torah like a boss. Maxie is still on her journey; when we go to grown-up services, I often let her bring a book. (She does not throw it on the ground or tear it into a dozen pieces.) She's still getting *something* out of being there. She enjoys services a lot more at her Jewish summer camp, when she's among a whole hut full of her peers, all singing their tiny hearts out. Camp has been, for me, the hidden weapon in making my kids spiritual and thoughtful. They go to unfancy, *haimish* (homey) camps that emphasize *tikkun olam*.

Grown-ups can keep learning spiritually too. When Josie had her Bat Mitzvah, she asked if I wanted to read Torah with her. I was terrified. I'd never done it before. At the time of my own Bat Mitzvah, the synagogue my parents belonged to didn't allow girls to read Torah. Today, that synagogue accords women and LGBT Jews the right to participate fully in ritual life in a way it didn't in the past. Institutions evolve too. (Alas, some rabbis, synagogues, and individuals still have a way to go.) I faced my fear and learned to read my portion. Touching the ancient, historic scroll, chanting timeless words in tune known to Jews all over the planet, taking part in something hugely significant to Jewish life and parental life felt momentous.

## ONE SIZE DOES NOT FIT ALL

We aren't all the same, and our experience of spirituality shouldn't be either. There are many ways to be in the world, and many ways to feel connected to God and humanity. For me, keeping kosher is a spiritual practice. A truly devout Jew would think me utterly half-assed. I insist on buying kosher meat, but don't care if my husband cooks bratwurst, his ancestral food. (He's from Wisconsin.) We have only one set of dishes, rather than a milk set and a meat set. I don't eat pork or shellfish, but don't care if anyone else in my family does. (They do.) I'm very interested in a new-ish movement called "ethical *kashrut*" (kashrut = the act of keeping kosher), which counts treating workers humanely and paying them fairly as fully essential as paying attention to how sharp the knives are and how clean the cut is and how unblemished the cows are. Paying workers less than minimum wage and providing lousy working conditions *should* be considered unkosher, even if the animals are ritually slaughtered in the "correct" way. I often think about throwing up my hands and simply buying free-range, organic, hormone-free meat, since the provenance is often easier to track and more trustworthy than that of kosher ethical meat. Why not just dispense with the kosher part? And yet I can't, because every time I eat I think about what my quixotic rules are, and they're a spiritual reminder of my Jewishness and the choices I make every day.

## SPIRITUALITY AND THE BODY

All of us can practice mindfulness in eating: listening to our own bodies' cues about hunger and satiety, thinking about the provenance of our food, being grateful for what we have. Think about food as a connection to the body, a way to nourish it. Further, think about how we move and treat our bodies as a way to feel wonder and miracles.

Elana Sztokman, an important Orthodox feminist thinker, is a far more religiously observant person than I, but I love what she has to say about the role of the corporeal self in feeling spiritually connected. "On Shabbat, in the *Birchot HaShachar* [morning blessings], we give thanks for what our bodies can do—walking, opening our eyes, waking up—and for having clothing for our bodies," she says. "This acknowledgement and appreciation of the body attracted me even more to Judaism, even though I'd struggled with my own body issues since childhood."

If you believe in God, think on how we all are created in the divine image, and thus deserving of love and respect. If you don't believe in God, well, think about the sheer wonderment and complexity of the human body. All religions carry the risk of excessive "rulesiness," a kind of nitpicky, snitty, letter-of-the-law obsessiveness. Spirituality can be a corrective to that. Sexuality, too, is part of appreciating your body—treating it carefully, wanting it to feel good, knowing it deserves pleasure and not sanction while also respecting the bodies of others.

And again, if you want to leave God out of the mix, go for it. A group known as Humanistic Jews, founded by a Reform-trained rabbi named Sherwin Wine in 1963, practices their own God-free variant of Judaism. Humanistic Jews identify with the history, culture, and future of the Jewish people; believe that no one group has a monopoly on chosenness; and feel that ethics and morality are about the here and now rather than about words passed down from on high by any Supreme Being or force. Meanwhile, Reconstructionist Jews and most Reform and Conservative Jews believe in a nonanthropomorphized notion of God. Reconstructionism's founder, Mordecai Kaplan (1881–1983), defined God as the human spirit that can "impel man to transcend himself . . . to rise above the brute and to eliminate all forms of violence and exploitation from human society." He called God "the Power in the cosmos that gives human life the direction that enables the human being to reflect the image of God."

In short: You can be religious and you can be spiritual without believing in the often vengeful, seemingly capricious God depicted in the Torah. Without believing in any other religious text, even! But being careful and kind to yourself and others—those things are not optional.

## TEACH GRATITUDE

Pointing out your kid's advantages and blessings is another way to foster healthy spirituality. Harvard's Making Caring Common Project cites studies showing that people who regularly express gratitude are more likely to be generous, compassionate, helpful, and forgiving. They're also more likely to be healthy and happy. The work of my Harvard classmate Sonja Lyubomirsky, a professor of psychology at the University of California, Riverside, has found that people who are consistently grateful have been found to be more energetic and more hopeful, and they report experiencing more frequent positive emotions. They also tend to be quicker to forgive and less materialistic than those who are less grateful.

One 2003 study asked people to count their blessings, literally. They were told to write down five things for which they were thankful. They did this once a week for ten weeks. Other groups of volunteers were asked to think about five hassles or five major events of the week. Compared to the control groups, the gratitude group felt more optimistic and satisfied with life after the study. They also felt better, with fewer headaches than the other two groups, and they spent more time exercising. Other studies have found that people who express gratitude tend to feel more interest and excitement in the world and more joy in their existence. They're more likely to report helping someone to feel connected with others, and they even sleep better.

What if we all made a conscious decision to *kvell* instead of *kvetch*? (Go look at the glossary already.) What if we focused on raising kids to be reflective and generous instead of hypercompetitive and grade-grubby? We might end up with kids who are both accomplished and amazing.

## Mamaleh Methodology

1. When kids are small, make righteousness a commandment, not a choice. Take kids with you to visit a friend in the hospital (they can say hi and then sit outside the room playing on your iPhone). Have them help you make sandwiches for hungry people and hand them out in a park. Collect little bottles of shampoo and body wash from hotels and frequent travelers and donate them to a shelter (first calling to be sure the shelter actually wants them). Older kids can lead coat drives, make string or lanyard bracelets to sell to raise money for charity, walk an elderly neighbor's dog when it's snowing out. Demand that all children say please and thank you.

2. Encourage children to bring peace between people. The Hebrew term for this is *Hava'at Shalom ben Adam l'Havero.* Help friends resolve an argument, choose not to throw a fit when your sibling borrows your jeans without asking, share

the lone remaining cookie rather than grabbing it and running cackling through the house while your sibling screams in rage.

3. **Care for the planet.** Kids love lecturing adults about environmentalism. God help you if you leave the water running while you brush your teeth. Channel your child's desire to feel superior to you by teaching the value of *Bal Tashkhit,* avoiding wastefulness. Participate in park and beach cleanups, make sure everything is properly thrown away and recycled at home and at school, donate seedlings from your backyard to a community garden, take nature walks to appreciate the world's wonders.

4. **Get involved in volunteer work, and let your kids know about it.** Show kids that service is an essential stand-alone value, not just a way to suck up to someone, make yourself feel noble, or buff up your résumé to get into college. (I have been a Harvard alumni interviewer and I have sat in on a season of Columbia admissions for a magazine story, and if I see one more college essay by a privileged white child about how they learned perspective from their volunteer trip to Guatemala, I will hit someone with a hacky sack.)

# How to Raise a Mensch

In the Bible, God talks to Elijah in a "still, small voice." In other ancient stories, God appears in a whirlwind, an earthquake, a fire. God is a drama queen, basically. But when God really wants to connect with Elijah, God speaks in a gentle whisper. This anecdote means, I think, that religion and parenting alike may seem like momentous, portentous subjects, yet *living them* doesn't mean a constant rush of revelation and miracles. Religion and parenting—the *actual doing* of religion and parenting—are about being quietly present, staying thoughtful, doing the day-to-day work of connection.

Not to sound like a Buddhist, but it's hard to live in the moment. That's the struggle with parenting. I'm in a perpetual fight with myself not to take moral shortcuts, not to give in to that piping kvetching whining little *yetzer-hara*-inflected voice (my kids' and my own!).

Our struggle as parents today isn't merely to keep our children alive, or smooth their way in the world. It's to keep our kids from becoming schmucks. Some of us are better at this than others; that's always been true. But historically, Jews have worked hard at raising non-dicks, and we've done pretty well for ourselves in the bargain. Follow our teachings and you may not get a Nobel Prize winner, but you'll definitely get a good human being. (And maybe also a Nobel Prize winner.)

There are legitimate reasons to worry that the factors that have made Jews so successful over time—our literacy, historical cluefulness, independence, discipline, geekiness, humor, flexibility, financial savvy, and spiritual discipline—are more at risk now than in the past. We American Jews are part of a long stretch of living in relative ease and comfort. Can we keep our edge and difference when there feels as though there's no compelling need to? Yet somehow . . . we do. At least thus far. Among Americans age sixty-five and older who say they had one Jewish parent, 25 percent are Jewish today. By contrast, among adults under thirty with one Jewish parent, 59 percent are Jewish today.

Intermarriage makes most Jewish leaders shriek like Donald Sutherland at the end of *Invasion of the Body Snatchers,* but we've had high rates of intermarriage before in our history. When people aren't surrounded by hate, they tend to marry outside their group. In our case, what with history being cyclical, Jews have always eventually gotten hated on again, circled the wagons, and then refocused on religion, ritual, faith, and culture. Not to be too much of a downer here, but the fact that anti-Semitic hate crimes are way up in Europe may indicate the beginning of a pendulum shift.

Regardless, Jews need to stop acting like this unprecedented crisis of Jewish identity is unprecedented. We are in a golden age of appreciating Jewish culture—Ashkenazic and Sephardic foods, Jewish music, a revival of interest in old Jewish languages, interest in Jewish history, literature, and art. While it's essential for us to tell stories and to share cultural and familial history, I'm not convinced that prayer and being surrounded only by people who are like you are utterly vital to identity. What Jewish mothers have always done is transmit values and stories. In a pluralistic world, we can share our own narratives and appreciate other people's.

Judaism needs to welcome everyone to our tent, just as our grandfather Abraham did. Ours is a rich, complex, tasty, mixed-up *cholent* or *shakshuka* (see, I picked an Ashkenazic *and* a Sephardic dish!) and if some people are more interested in religion and others are more interested in culture, well, we have both.

Whatever your faith tradition—and indeed, even if you have none—I hope that books and storytelling will continue to create common ground for us all. I hope you'll choose to use the mothering strategies that have imbued Jewish kids with the ethics and drive to become accomplished, kind *mensches*. I hope the values and savvy that have worked so well in the past—helping Jewish mothers mold iconoclastic, independent, creative, successful, empathetic people—will continue to shape us for generations, even as the world continues to change. As it always has, and always will.

# YOUR YIDDISH GLOSSARY

*(You should only enjoy!)*

BALABOOSTA: Supercompetent housewife/home manager

BUBBE: Grandma

BUPKES: Zip, zilch, zero

CHALERIA: Insanely anxious fidgety person (literally "a person with cholera")

CHUTZPAH: Chutzpah (Oh, FINE: It means boldness, spunk, pushiness.)

FARKLEMPT: Choked up

FARSHTUNKINER: Godforsaken

GOY/GOYIM: Non-Jewish person. Not an insult; literally means "people" or "nation."

HAIMISH: Nice and homey

HOCK: Noodge

KIBITZ: Chat; see Schmooze

# YOUR YIDDISH GLOSSARY

KREPLACH: A tasty dumpling; basically, a wonton, gyoza, momo, or raviolo, but Jewish

KVELL: Express deep pride

KVETCH: Complain (literally "squeeze, press," from the German *quetsche*, "crusher")

MACHER: A big-shot muckety-muck wheeler-dealer power broker

MENSCH: Literally "man," but in general usage, a good human being

MIDRASH: Exegesis, the interpretive process of trying to answer questions about Torah and religion

MISHEGAS: Craziness

MITZVAH: Literally "commandment," but also used to mean "good deed"; plural is "mitzvot"

NOODGE: Hock, push (It literally means "pester," from the Yiddish *nudyen*.)

PESACH: Passover, the holiday that commemorates the Hebrews' escape from slavery under Pharaoh in Egypt. Traditionally Jews hold a Seder, a long but delightful meal in which the story of liberation is retold and parallels to modern tyranny are drawn and children are indulged.

PIRKEI AVOT: *Ethics of the Fathers,* a text that addresses moral behavior

POGROM: Organized massacre of Jews in Eastern European shtetls

SCHMOOZE: See Kibitz

SEDER: Passover meal with lots of ritual involved; can involve fun masks and toys and throwing marshmallows at each other while calling them a plague of hail

SHEYGITZ: Boy shiksa. (Do not use. Shiksa and sheygitz are not nice words.)

SHIKSA: Non-Jewish woman. Pejorative; literally means "unclean thing." The male equivalent is "sheygitz."

SHPILKES: A bouncy state of agitation (literally "needles")

SHTETL: Jewish ghetto, or small Jewish village in Eastern Europe before the Holocaust

SUKKOT: The annual harvest festival, when we eat and sometimes sleep in outdoor huts called *sukkot* (one hut is a *sukkah*)

TALMUD: An important collection of rabbinic teachings and interpretations of Torah, compiled between the first and seventh centuries CE

TIKKUN OLAM: Healing the world

TORAH: The Five Books of Moses, the Pentateuch, what some Christians call the Old Testament

TUCHUS: Butt, bum, tush (like *tuchus, tush* is from the Hebrew *tachat,* which means "under"), fundament, glutes, dat ass, caboose, badonkadonk

TZEDAKAH: Literally "righteousness," but often used to mean "charity"

VONTZ: Annoying person (literally "bedbug")

YESHIVA: A school, generally Orthodox, focused on the study of traditional religious texts

ZAYDE: Grandfather

---

(Note: A few of these words—like *sukkot* and *tikkun olam*—are straight-up Hebrew, not Yiddish. Don't get all *farblonget* [disturbed] about it, okay?)

# FOR FURTHER READING

Aboab, Isaac, and Yaakov Yosef Reinman. *Menoras Hamaor.* Lakewood, NJ (674 8th St., Lakewood 08701): Y. Reinman, 1982.

Antler, Joyce. *You Never Call! You Never Write! A History of the Jewish Mother.* Oxford: Oxford University Press, 2007.

Baum, Charlotte, and Paula Hyman. *The Jewish Woman in America.* New York: Dial Press, 1976.

Bazelon, Emily. *Sticks and Stones: Defeating the Culture of Bullying and Rediscovering the Power of Character and Empathy.* New York: Random House, 2013.

Bronson, Po, and Ashley Merryman. *NurtureShock: New Thinking about Children.* New York: Twelve, 2009.

Brumberg, Joan Jacobs. *The Body Project: An Intimate History of American Girls.* New York: Random House, 1997.

Coles, Robert. *The Call of Service: A Witness to Idealism.* Boston: Houghton Mifflin, 1993.

Drehle, David Von. *Triangle: The Fire That Changed America.* New York: Atlantic Monthly, 2003.

Foer, Franklin, and Marc Tracy. *Jewish Jocks: An Unorthodox Hall of Fame*. New York: Twelve, 2012.

Goldstein, Phyllis. *A Convenient Hatred: The History of Antisemitism*. Brookline, MA: Facing History and Ourselves, 2012.

Greenburg, Dan. *How to Be a Jewish Mother: A Very Lovely Training Manual*. Los Angeles: Price, Stern, Sloan; Distributed by Pocket Books [New York], 1964.

Greengrass, Linda, ed. *The Best Books to Read Aloud with Children of All Ages*. New York: Bank Street College of Education, 2012.

Handelman, Susan, and Ora Wiskind Elper, eds. *Torah of the Mothers*. New York: Urim Publications, 2000.

*The Memoirs of Glückel of Hameln*. New York: Schocken Books, 1977.

Heschel, Abraham Joshua. *Moral Grandeur and Spiritual Audacity: Essays*. New York: Farrar, Straus & Giroux, 1996.

Howe, Irving. *Jewish-American Stories*. New York: New American Library, 1977.

Hyman, Paula. *Gender and Assimilation in Modern Jewish History: The Roles and Representation of Women*. Seattle: University of Washington Press, 1995.

Himmelfarb, Gertrude. *The People of the Book: Philosemitism in England, from Cromwell to Churchill*. New York: Encounter Books, 2011.

Ingall, Carol K., ed. *The Women Who Reconstructed American Jewish Education, 1910–1965*. Waltham, MA: Brandeis University Press, 2010.

Jacobs, Jill. *Where Justice Dwells: A Hands-on Guide to Doing Social Justice in Your Jewish Community*. 2011 Quality Pbk. ed. Woodstock, VT: Jewish Lights, 2011.

Joselit, Jenna Weissman. *The Wonders of America: Reinventing Jewish Culture 1880–1950*. New York: Hill and Wang, 1994.

Kay, Devra. *Seyder Tkhines: The Forgotten Book of Common Prayer for Jewish Women*. Philadelphia: Jewish Publication Society, 2004.

Klapper, Melissa R. *Ballots, Babies, and Banners of Peace: American Jewish Women's Activism, 1890–1940*. New York: NYU Press, 2014.

Kobliner, Beth. *Make Your Kid a Money Genius (Even If You're Not)*. New York: Simon & Schuster, 2016.

Lieber, Ron. *The Opposite of Spoiled: Raising Kids Who Are Grounded, Generous, and Smart about Money*. New York: Harper, 2015.

Lyubomirsky, Sonja. *The How of Happiness: A Scientific Approach to Getting the Life You Want*. New York: Penguin Press, 2008.

Marcus, Jacob Rader. *The American Jewish Woman: A Documentary History*. New York: Ktav, 1981.

Markel, Michelle, and Melissa Sweet. *Brave Girl: Clara and the Shirtwaist Makers' Strike of 1909*. New York: Balzer + Bray, 2013.

Miller, Donalyn. *The Book Whisperer: Awakening the Inner Reader in Every Child*. San Francisco: Jossey-Bass, 2009.

Naumberg, Carla. *Parenting in the Present Moment: How to Stay Focused on What Really Matters*. Berkeley, CA: Parallax Press, 2014.

Ner-David, Haviva. *Chanah's Voice: A Rabbi Wrestles with Gender, Commandment, and the Women's Rituals of Baking, Bathing, and Brightening*. Teaneck, NJ: Ben Yehuda Press, 2013.

Nuland, Sherwin B. *Maimonides*. New York: Nextbook, 2005.

Orenstein, Peggy. *Cinderella Ate My Daughter: Dispatches from the Front Lines of the New Girlie-Girl Culture*. New York: Harper, 2011.

Prell, Riv-Ellen. *Fighting to Become Americans: Jews, Gender, and the Anxiety of Assimilation*. Boston: Beacon Press, 1999.

Prinz, Deborah R. *On the Chocolate Trail: A Delicious Adventure Connecting Jews, Religions, History, Travel, Rituals and Recipes to the Magic of Cacao.* Woodstock, VT: Jewish Lights Publ., 2013.

Riley, Naomi Schaefer. *'Til Faith Do Us Part: How Interfaith Marriage Is Transforming America.* Oxford, England: Oxford University Press, 2013.

Ripley, Amanda. *The Smartest Kids in the World and How They Got That Way.* New York: Simon & Schuster, 2013.

Rosenberg, Shelley Kapnek, Ed.D. *Raising a Mensch: How to Bring Up Ethical Children in Today's World.* Philadelphia: Jewish Publication Society, 2003.

Schama, Simon. *The Story of the Jews: Finding the Words: 1000 BC–1492 AD.* New York: Ecco, 2014.

Telushkin, Joseph. *Jewish Humor: What the Best Jewish Jokes Say about the Jews.* New York: W. Morrow, 1992.

Umansky, Ellen M., and Dianne Ashton. *Four Centuries of Jewish Women's Spirituality: A Sourcebook.* Boston: Beacon Press, 1992.

Weinberg, Sydney Stahl. *The World of Our Mothers: The Lives of Jewish Immigrant Women.* Chapel Hill: University of North Carolina Press, 1988.

Zheutlin, Peter. *Around the World on Two Wheels: Annie Londonderry's Extraordinary Ride.* New York: Citadel Press, 2007.

# ACKNOWLEDGMENTS

When Josie was four, she went through a phase of refusing to say "please," "thank you," or "I'm sorry." I'd insist. She'd balk. It was Politeness Battle Royale. One day I prompted her to say "please" and she replied, "I'm saying 'please' in my head." I answered, "It doesn't *count* to say it in your head. For something to actually be polite, people actually have to hear it." She replied. "You *did* hear it. I said 'please' when I said 'I said "please" in my head.'"

In that spirit, please forgive me if I haven't thanked you by name in these acknowledgments. You are fabulous, and I thank you in my head.

That said, a thank-you out loud goes to my agent, Sarah Burnes, and to my editor, Heather Jackson. Sarah is the perfect mix of hand-holding and badass, and Heather is an astute, savvy, whip-cracking truth teller. Thank you, too, to Michele Eniclerico, Lauren Cook, and Stephanie Davis at Harmony, who graciously put up with my *shpilkes*. I would also like to thank my cover designer, Elena Giavaldi, and illustrator, Luci Gutiérrez. I was sad when the lovely Leah Miller, who acquired *Mamaleh,* left for a new gig, but I couldn't have asked for a better publishing experience.

This book wouldn't exist without Gayle Forman, my Charlotte the Spider—wonderful friend, wonderful writer. Fortunately, she continues to encourage me and laugh with me, and she has not left me with an egg sac.

Thanks to my magazine and newspaper editors past and present, for bringing me up in the way that I should go, which I can't say in Yiddish but would if I could. Biggest thanks to Alana Newhouse, for hiring me at *Tablet,* and to Wayne Hoffman, who is a brilliant editor, a soothing presence, and a true mensch.

Thank you to Rita Ali, our babysitter when the kids were little. She was a blessing to all of us. Much love and gratitude to Jonathan, who picked up the slack while I was writing this damn thing and made delicious, delicious meat. Mortifyingly effusive hugs to Josie and Maxie, who dealt with my frequent disappearances to work and did not go feral. I love you. You amuse me and make me proud every day. Always laugh and sing and make music.

# INDEX

# ABOUT THE AUTHOR

MARJORIE INGALL is a columnist for *Tablet Magazine,* the National Magazine Award–winning journal of Jewish culture and ideas, and a regular contributor to *The New York Times Book Review.* For seven years she wrote the East Village Mamele column for *The Jewish Daily Forward.* She has been a contributing editor at *Glamour* and a contributing writer at *Self,* and has written for *Real Simple, Ms., Wired, Redbook, Parents,* and the late, lamented *Sassy,* where she was a senior writer and the books editor. She is the author of *The Field Guide to North American Males* and coauthor (with the model Crystal Renn) of *Hungry.* She is a former senior writer and producer at the Oxygen TV network, where she discovered her perkiness levels were not sufficient for a job in daytime talk television. She lives in New York City's East Village with her husband, children, and two vocal cats.